Keeper of the Greens

Keeper of the Greens

Larry Runyon

Writers Club Press
San Jose New York Lincoln Shanghai

Keeper of the Greens

Writers Club Press
an imprint of iUniverse.com, Inc.

For information address:
iUniverse.com, Inc.
5220 S 16th, Ste. 200
Lincoln, NE 68512
www.iuniverse.com

ISBN: 0-595-18388-3

Printed in the United States of America

This book is dedicated to Sue, my High School sweetheart and wife of over 40 years and to our three great kids, Rhonda, Larry Paul and Robin. This is their life, too.

Forward

Whitey Ford
Comments on Larry Runyon's
Keeper of the Greens

I have known some characters in my time and Larry Runyon is definitely one of them. I have known some storytellers in my time and Larry is one of the best. I have known some innovative thinkers in my time and Larry is one of the most inventive problem solvers I've ever known. I have had some great friends in my time and Larry is certainly numbered among those.

As I read his memoirs, *Keeper of the Greens,* I was struck by how American his story is. Born into modest circumstances, afflicted by a frightening disease, beneficiary of a modest education, he rose above his circumstances and has succeeded. He became an accomplished golfer. He learned by improvising and observing. He never quit. Today he is part of a company that is revolutionizing how golf courses and agriculture handle disease, pests and growth… all without chemicals. And most of it comes from Larry's patents.

Everyone should read this book. It is about the triumph of the human spirit. The success of the common man. The overcoming of tremendous obstacles. *Keeper of the Greens* is also one of the funniest books you will read in a long time.

Whitey Ford

Preface

I would imagine that most people find their own life story pretty interesting and I'm no exception. The thing that I find sort of curious is that most other folks find it interesting, too! Looking back I guess it is something to be proud of. I went from a being a polio afflicted kid in a dusty town on the Kansas plains to being a golf professional, to one of the highest paid golf course superintendents in the business, and finally to the holder of patents that will revolutionize the golf course maintenance industry as well as the agricultural industry. Not bad for a guy with very little formal education.

What follows are stories about my travels, jobs and life that I have either lived through, influenced or observed over the past sixty years. They are all true and only an occasional name change was required to protect the guilty and sometimes the innocent.

Acknowledgements

I just can't let you read any further without knowing about my buddy Chuck Fox. You see he is this ol' country editor and semi-professional Irishman that did his best to listen to all my stories, fill in some blanks and edit it all into what you have in your hands. He and I have shared more than a few lemonades, laughs and almost a car crash and lived to tell about it. Thanks, buddy.

Chapter 1

Folks say that there were two world-class clowns born in Sedan, Kansas. One was a guy named Emmett Kelly who hung out with the Ringling Brothers and Barnum and Bailey Circus. He was kind of a sad faced ol' boy who had a knack for making people laugh.

The other clown was me, Larry Runyon. Now I can't remember a sober time when I painted up my face but I could always make folks laugh pretty good. I couldn't help it, really, I just sort of saw funny things happening around me. It's been that way my whole life. Especially since I've spent nearly my whole life in the sometimes strange, sometimes hilarious and always enjoyable world of golf. I've spent 40 odd years hanging around country clubs in one capacity or another and I've seen it all.

As I said, Emmett Kelly and I were both born in the pretty southeast Kansas town of Sedan. It sits down in a valley that the Indians prophesized would prevent a tornado from ever touching down. So far they've been right. When I was growing up the town was lined with beautiful elm trees. The Dutch Elm Disease that came through in the 1950's nearly wiped out every one of them, but it was a pretty place when I was a kid. It was mostly a farming community with a few oil wells spotted around. It was the county seat of Chautauqua County and a real friendly place. For years, when my folks would go out of town, they never bothered to lock the doors. I remember there was one movie theater on one of the big, wide main streets of town. It was the Gregg Theater for a while and then it was called the Chief. One Saturday afternoon, while we were watching Roy Rogers, my next door neighbor, George Casement, threw a rock at a bad guy on the screen and took his head right off, tearing the screen. He was only trying to protect Roy, but he got himself banned from the Gregg until it was sold and renamed the Chief.

For years there were two major highways that converged just outside of town and then separated on the other side of town. Not long ago they built a big interstate highway that sort of bypassed Sedan. Even before the bypass the Mayor, Ernie Meadows, and the Chamber of Commerce decided that the town needed some sort of a tourist attraction to entice motorists to spend more time, and money, in Sedan. Someone came up with the idea to erect a big ol' sign out on the highway proclaiming Sedan to be the birthplace of Emmett Kelly. Sure enough, folks started coming into town and asking where Emmett had lived. The townspeople pointed out a certain house and folks took pictures and left happy. Pretty soon the town fathers decided that it would be appropriate to purchase the house and turn it into an Emmett Kelly museum. As soon as they let it be known what they had in mind, the price of real estate went up! After about a year of haggling the deal is done and Emmett starts to send them all kinds of mementos and souvenirs and memorabilia to put into the house. When they finally get it all fixed up and ready to go, they invited Emmett Kelly to town for the dedication. As they are standing in front of the museum Kelly punches Mayor Meadows in the side and whispers, "Hey, Mayor, I wasn't born in that one, I was born in the house across the street!" The Mayor turns beet red and chokes out "Jesus Christ! Don't tell anyone!" Until now nobody did. The two highways that converged in Sedan made it a fairly prosperous place. The streets were wide and, like I said, lined with big ol' elm trees. It was a good, solid mid-western farm town with good, solid mid-western people you could count on, as I came to find out first hand.

If I was born to be a golfer, that promise seemed to end when I was two and a half years old. That's when I became one of the one percent of the pre-Salk Vaccine children to contract Poliomyelitis. I was luckier than some, though. Especially lucky to be a boy in those days. You see the theory at the time was to vigorously pull and stretch the affected muscles. As a consequence they were much more rigorous on the boys than the girls because they were afraid to be too tough on the girls since it was felt that they were more delicate and subject to being injured. It turned out years later that the strenuous workout was exactly the right thing to do and the boys generally came through the experience in better shape. They called it the Sister Kenny program and it involved hot towels and a lot of pulling and stretching. I remember a few boys getting their leg or arm broken, but I don't recall ever hearing of a girl being injured. A lot of kids in there were abandoned because their folks either couldn't afford treatment or couldn't face the consequences of the disease. I was in Wesley Hospital in Wichita, Kansas because my folks couldn't afford it but the KCC, the Kansas Crippled Children's Committee, took me in and provided for my care. I'm grateful to them to this day. I survived and was able to walk without crutches. To this day I walk with a limp and wear a brace but it hasn't hurt my golf game any.

I remember that my mother used to take me to the hospital in Wichita on a bus. It was 100 miles and because of the war many people didn't have gas rations or tires for their cars so they rode the bus. Buses were just jam packed in those days and my mother would stand up, holding me, the entire trip to and from Wichita. I don't remember anyone ever offering her their seat. Later on, when we finally got a car and some gas rations, we had a terrible time with the synthetic rubber tires and tubes that were in use because the rubber was needed for the war effort. My mom carried the necessary tools to jack up the car, take the tire off, pull out the tube, patch it up, and use a hand pump to inflate it and put it back on. Because the quality of those synthetics was so bad, an average trip to Wichita involved an average of 15 tire repairs along the way. Another draw back of the synthetics was that you could only drive a maximum of 35 MPH on them. The wealthy, of course, could afford real rubber tires and would glide along at 50 MPH or so which seemed real fast at the time. My dad worked for a gentleman by the name of Dingbell who owned the local Chevy dealership. One day my sister Marylyn and I were riding with mom and Mrs. Dingbell came roaring past us. We all wished that she would have a blowout. About three miles farther on we had the blowout! My mom patched the tire with a piece of the spare, which we had ruined earlier, and a spare tube that she carried and we made it home by going no more that 15 MPH to whole way. I didn't realize it at the time, but she was and still is an amazing woman.

Actually, Polio is the reason I got into golf in the first place. As a kid, I was interested in anything that would give me walking exercise. There in Sedan we had a little nine hole, sand green, private country club golf course and I would slip under the fence and play the back few holes. Now I only had one old beat up club that I found in Al Wickham's barn, hanging up on a hook. He didn't play golf and I think that he must have found this old wood-shafted driver somewhere and hung it up there. His son, Tom, was in my class in school and neither one of them had any interest in golf so they gave me that old driver.

At the time, about 1949 or '50, kids just weren't allowed to play golf, especially at private country clubs. So I would slip under the fence along the sixth fairway and bat the ball around. I got run off a good many times and finally I made the mistake of sneaking onto the course on a Sunday morning. As I was sliding under the fence, the local undertaker, Riley Buckles grabbed me by the scruff of the neck and hauled me back to the clubhouse. He asked the waiting members "What the hell are we going to do with this kid?" Most of the members just laughed, but one of the founders of the club, Clyde Denman, who was a wealthy oil man, said "I'll tell you what we're going to do with him, we're going to make him a member and his dues are going to be $5 and here's his first year's dues in advance!"

Now Clyde had a son named Walter who was in his forties at the time and had a wooden leg. He was recognized nationally as a champion amputee golfer. The Denman family took me under their wing, taught me how to play and took me all around the country to play golf. It was an educational experience, and a lot of fun, but it had its embarrassing moments, too. Walter once took me on the train up to see the Kansas City

Open, which was a big tournament in those days. I was about 13 years old and this was an awe-inspiring outing to see the big name golfers of the day. On Saturday of the tournament, we were standing next to the ninth green and Dr. Cary Middlecoff was crouched over a putt. Now the good doctor was a notoriously slow putter and he was camped over this putt for what seemed like 45 minutes. Finally Walter lets out with a booming fart that seemed to echo around the course. Everyone around the green looked in our direction and Walter turned to me and said, "Runyon, you shouldn't have done that!" and walked away. Suddenly I was standing all alone and Dr. Cary Middlecoff is glaring at me. I got out of there as quick as I could and when I found Walter I didn't say a word to him. Not the rest of the afternoon, not that night at dinner, not on the train ride home the next day. Not a word. Of course he said plenty when we got back to the club. He couldn't wait to tell the story. It was soon all around town and to this day there are old boys around that town who love to tell the tale of when young Runyon farted Cary Middlecoff away from a putt.

I was somewhat of an oddity at the time because kids, especially kids with polio, just didn't play golf. I really got into it. I'd play all year around, even in the snow. I had a great ambition to be a professional golfer. I played the Sedan course everyday when I wasn't traveling with the Denman family and kept it up until I was about sixteen years old. That's when I discovered airplanes. I learned from the crop dusters out at the airfield. From that time on I had two ambitions. One was professional golf and the other was to be a crop duster. I loved to fly.

Shortly after learning to fly, I almost learned to crash. I was just 17 years old at the time and I had stupidly had a couple of beers before I went up. I just got over Hula Dam, just south of Sedan, when I discovered that I had to pee. I was flying a J-3 Cub with the sides off since it was summer time. I figured that if I got the plane trimmed up and flying straight and level, I could unbuckle and hang my feet out of the cockpit, on the struts. I sort of stood up, unzipped and started to pee into Hula Lake. That's when I hit the down draft! That is also when I fell out of the airplane!

Luckily I grabbed on to the strut and hung on for dear life. With my weight out on the wing like that, the plane goes into a tight, right hand spiral. I scrambled to get back into the cockpit, not so much because I thought I could pull out of the dive, but to get my pants zipped up! I thought that I was going to die and I didn't want to be found with my fly open. I managed to get inside, zip up and I pulled up with about 20 feet to spare! It was incidents like this that led, many years later, to an Indian tribe to name me Chief Little Bladder.

During this time I was in high school and I was working as a welder for McCunningham Tank Company that was owned by Archie McCunningham. It was there that I became a certified welder before I was eighteen years old. It was also about this time that I met the lovely Sue Kennedy. Now I wasn't the quickest lad in town, but I knew that Sue wasn't going to be around long if I didn't move fast. At the time I wore my hair kind of long because I had known this gal, Juanita Cole, who was a hairdresser in town and she and I had been taking flying lessons at the same place. At the time it was very unusual for women to be pilots, but then Juanita was not a usual kind of girl! One day she had told me that my hair was at a length that it should either be cut or she'd have to give me a permanent. I was fairly adventuresome, so I said, "Let's do it!" and off we went. Well it turned out pretty good and that is how I wore my hair when I met Sue. I guess she must have liked it because we ended up getting married. We had been married about six weeks when the perm starts to fade. Sue looks at my hair and asks what's wrong? I told her that nothing was wrong, I just needed a perm. She says, "You mean that's not natural? You look like hell! What ever you've been doing, go do it!" So off I go to see the lovely Juanita. This goes on for about a year until Sue meets the lovely Juanita. My hair has been in a flat top ever since!

You've got to understand that folks tended to marry at an early age in farm towns in those days. We'd been going together a while and when I was eighteen and Sue was fourteen, we went and got our license and headed for Molene, Kansas. Sue wanted to be married by a preacher rather than a Justice of the Peace and we stopped at several small churches, none of which had a preacher at home. It turns out that there was a preacher's convention going on in Independence, Kansas and all of the preachers were down there at the time. We finally came upon this little country church with a light on and sure enough, the preacher was at home and said he'd be happy to marry us. Inside the church there was the preacher, two old maid ladies and a three-legged dog. As the preacher gets along into the ceremony, this three-legged dog wanders between Sue and I and I nudge Sue and point out that the dog only has three legs. "Oh, yeah." Says the preacher and launches into this long and elaborate story about how the dog lost his leg. After awhile he runs out of steam and kind of looks around and asks, "Where was I?" Well none of us could remember exactly where in the proceedings he had been when he had taken off on his story so he says, "Ah, hell, let's start over!" So as near as Sue and I can tell, we may have been married twice! Must have been a pretty good job, though, because 42 years later we're still laughing about a country preacher, two old maids and a three legged dog!(Click here to input the text of your first chapter or other division.)

Chapter 2

When Sue and I got married, I took a job as an apprentice crop duster in Pratt, Kansas. A medium sized town of about 20,000; Pratt is right smack dab in the middle of wheat country, flat as a pancake, no trees. The wind blows nearly every day. The people are friendly and hard working. It is a typical mid-western town.

Sue stayed in Sedan until school was out and I went ahead to Pratt to get us set up and start my job. Our home was to be in the loft of an old B-29 hangar at the airfield. I had told Sue that she would really like this place. I had taken the job sight unseen and when I got out to the field I was surprised to find that the B-29 loft was filled with 4,700 school desks. I spent my evenings hauling school desks down stairs and leaving them for the owners to find places to store them. All this time I repeatedly asked where the bathroom was in my loft. Everyone repeatedly assured me that it was behind the school desks. Sue arrived before I could get all of the desks out and she asked first thing where the bathroom was. I confidently assured her that it was behind the school desks. It took about another week of hauling school desks down stairs before we discovered that there was no bathroom. I was off to a really great start at married life.

I spent that whole season flying up and down the field, spraying water. The only insects that I killed were on the windshield of my plane. We were there a couple of months when we decided that we would really like to take a trip back home to Sedan, but we didn't have any money. After thinking it over, I came up with a terrific idea to pay for our trip. Several years before some old farmer had tried to grow onions between the runways. It didn't work out, but there was still a good batch of onions growing there. I told Sue that we would harvest the onions and sell them to the folks back home. She thought that was a pretty good idea, so we drove the car out to the field and filled the trunk up with onions and then we started throwing them in the back seat and filled that up to the roof and then we put them in the passenger seat. I told Sue that the more onions that we could fit in the more money we would make. It suddenly occurred to us that Sue needed someplace to sit, so I had her climb in the driver's side and then I pushed her in on top of the pile on the passenger side. I squeezed in behind the wheel and down the road we went, one hundred and sixty five miles to Sedan, Kansas. We hadn't gone much more than twenty miles when my eyes start to water so bad that I can't see straight. I began weaving all over the road and we get stopped by the Highway Patrol. It turns out that we knew the officer and he gets within a few feet of the car and he gasps for breath and walks to the other side of the highway. He yells across to us to start throwing out the onions in the front seat. When we got the load down to his satisfaction, we continued on to Sedan. We approached everyone in town, but we never sold one onion. Seems folks were growing their own or something, but they sure didn't have any interest in our onions. A year later, when I traded the car off, the buyer sniffed and asked if he smelled onions. I told him that I couldn't imagine why he would.

After the season was over, so was my job, so we moved back to Sedan. We found a little three-room house next to an airport hanger and I continued to build up my hours flying. Now, Sue's mom and dad lived up the road in Howard, Kansas and her dad and I spent many an afternoon nursing a beer and speculating as to whether or not a good pilot could land a plane on the main drag of Howard. It was a really wide street and there weren't too many wires running across it and I always figured that I could probably do it. One Saturday night we were at a dance with Sue's folks and I agreed to fly up the next morning and go fishing with her dad. I was supposed to buzz the house about six in the morning and he would come out to meet me. I got there right on time and circled the house and no one came out. So I circled a little lower and still no response. So I naturally got to thinking that since it was Sunday morning and no one would be around, I just might go over to Main Street and hang a wheelie in the middle of town. I lined up perfectly and dropped right down in the middle of the street and flew the length of town, right on the deck. When I pulled up and looked back, I couldn't see the town for all of the dust. I made a beeline for Sedan, thirty-five miles away. I got half way home and I could still see that dust cloud rising over Howard. I landed at the airstrip and hollered for Sue to bring some wet towels. I knew there was a better than even chance that I was going to get a visit from the Civil Air Patrol. We cooled the engine down and pushed the plane back into the corner of the hangar and waited. Sure enough, pretty soon the local CAP officer shows up. It turns out that it is a neighbor of Sue's dad. This guy loved his position of authority. He had double spotlights on his car, badges on his jacket and on his shirt and a CAP hat. The first thing he does is go and feel the engine on my plane. He came to me with a bewildered look on his face and said that he just knew that it had been me buzzing the town, but he hadn't gotten my numbers. He kept a pretty close eye on me after that, but he never caught me.

While we were living there next to the airstrip we became acquainted with most of the field mouse population of the area. We would sit in the living room at night and watch them scurry across the floor and down the furnace. One night we counted 270 field mice. We soon moved into a nice little apartment in town.

I resumed my job welding at McCunningham Tank Company shortly after moving back to town. One day not long after I started, I was outside welding in 100-degree heat when I decided that there had to be something better to do for a living. I turned off my torch and went to the foreman, a great guy by the name of Lud Brooks. I told him that I quit. He asked me what I was going to do for a living. I said that I didn't know, but it sure as hell wasn't going to be a welder.

I went home and told Sue what I had done and she asked me if I knew that we had exactly $1.75 in the bank. I said that I didn't think that we had that much. She asked what I was going to do and I said that they had built a new country club over in Coffeyville, Kansas that I had never played and I was going to go over and play it. And that's what I did. There were three guys on the first tee when I got there and I knew two of them and they asked me to join them. As we played along, one of the guys asked me what I did for a living these days. I said that as of 10:30 that morning I was unemployed. He told me that they had fired the Golf Pro the night before and suggested that I apply for the position of Golf Pro/Greenskeeper. I did just that after we finished the round. In the interview I admitted that I didn't know anything about taking care of grass greens. They allowed that there was an old boy by the name of Bob Dunning out of Tulsa, Oklahoma and if you buy all of your fertilizer and chemicals from him, he'll come up and teach all you need to know. I told them that it was fine with me. I went back home and three days later they called and said that the job was mine. Now in those days country clubs couldn't afford to hire a head pro and a

greenskeeper, so one guy did both jobs. This was the start of my education into turf grass management and a search for ways to use less and less chemicals and more organics. As you will see, I've been fairly successful at it. I should say right here that the term "greenskeeper" is hardly used anymore. Since the advent of the Golf Course Superintendents Association, greenskeepers prefer to be referred to as "Superintendents". It is a professional designation that we take a lot of pride in.

Sue and I made our third move of our married life to Coffeyville and moved into a spare room that an old lady had for rent. Exactly one hour and forty-five minutes later, Sue and I made the fourth move of our married life when the former Golf Pro stopped by and suggested that we might like to move into the place that he had been living in. His place was nicer, neater and, most importantly, cheaper than the one we had just moved into, so we moved again.

Coffeyville is a town of about 7,000 in southeast Kansas, right on the Oklahoma line. The town is most famous for the Dalton gang raid and there is a Dalton Gang Museum that folks like to stop by. Located among rolling hills, at the time we were there elm trees predominated the landscape, but the Dutch Elm Disease wiped them out in the 1950's. That whole area has some of the worst weather I've ever encountered— humidity high enough to wilt a starched shirt during the summer and wind chill cold enough to make an Eskimo shiver in the winter.

It was about this time that we had our first child, Rhonda. Sue was working as my assistant in the Pro Shop and we would leave for the course at 5:00AM, drop Rhonda off at my Aunt Belle's, go down to the ice company, buy a block of ice and head for the course. We would put the ice in the icebox to keep the beer and soft drinks cold.

At the time we had a plate in the icebox so that if Sue or I weren't there, members could leave money and take what they wanted on the honor system. After about a month of this, Sue came to me and said that the members were stealing us blind. I asked what she meant by that and she said that she had been doing inventory and there wasn't anywhere near enough money in the dish to cover the cost of the beer and soda. I told her that I saw her drinking an occasional Pepsi and asked if she was paying for those. She said that she wasn't. She said that she saw me drink an occasional beer, was I paying for those? I allowed that I wasn't. So we devised a system to keep track of our consumption. We kept a tally sheet and we would each make a mark each time we took a Pepsi or a beer. At the end of the first day Sue had 23 marks and I had 24. It's a good thing that we didn't complain to the members!

In those days I had one helper besides Sue and I was responsible for all of the course maintenance, mowing the greens and fairways, raking the traps and fertilizing everything. All of this was in addition to my duties as head pro. I would water the greens at night, after the last foursome had finished. Sue and I wouldn't get home, usually, until midnight or so after picking up Rhonda, and then we were right back at it at 5:00AM the next morning. For this I was getting paid the princely sum of $200 a month.

There were other compensations that made my time in Coffeyville worthwhile. One was the education that I got from Mr. Bob Dunning who at that time was recognized as one of the pioneers of bent grass golf courses in the mid-west. About once a month he would show up on a Sunday morning to see how I was doing. This one Sunday he arrives and we go out to inspect the course and we get up on a hill next to the sixth green where we had a big old water tank and some drinking cups. We both took a couple of cups full and headed back to the pro shop. I hadn't yet put the block of ice into the cooler and as I stooped to pick it up I crapped in my drawers! Then when I started toward the cooler, I stepped in a depression and crapped in my drawers again! As I lifted the ice into the cooler, I did it a third time! I was standing there trying to figure out what was happening to me when Bob comes up and says that I would have to take him back to the clubhouse because he had just crapped in his drawers. I asked him how many times? He says once. I tell him I'm two up on him. We jump in an old pick up truck that we used around the course and head for the clubhouse. Every time we hit a pothole, we crap again. By the time we get there I'm still one up on him. When we get into the locker room we see the place filled with golfers who have the same problem. I find out that the women's locker room is the same way. One of the members was a doctor and he suggested that he take a sample of the drinking water and have it tested. When the results came back he said that there was enough Crotin Oil in the water to give every citizen in Coffeyville diarrhea for three days. Crotin Oil is a laxative used for horses. Nobody ever confessed and we never did find out who laced the water tank, but we did put a lock and chain on it after that.

It was about this time that one of the members had a St. Bernard that he couldn't keep fed. He asked me if I wanted to keep him out at the course and I jumped at the offer. I had always wanted a St. Bernard. I figured that we could keep him happy with the table scraps from the club restaurant. I learned that I was mistaken the Tuesday after his arrival. There was a ladies tournament that morning and just before I saw the first foursome finish I saw the St. Bernard come around the corner of the clubhouse with a full filet in his mouth and the chef right behind him with a butcher knife in his hand. Now this chef was a huge, heavyset old boy and I had no idea that he could run as fast as he did. He caught the dog about halfway down the first fairway and wrestled the filet out of his mouth. Later that day I was supposed to hand out the trophies to the winners of the ladies tournament at their luncheon. When I walked into the room, I saw that they were enjoying a filet lunch with all of the trimmings. They asked if I would like to join them and I begged off saying that I had had a big breakfast. I just know that 8 or 10 of them were enjoying the very same cuts that the St. Bernard had enjoyed a few hours earlier. That big old dog disappeared shortly after that. I never did find out what happened to him.

One of the big events that happened while I was in Coffeyville was the Kansas State Junior Chamber of Commerce Golf Tournament. Shortly before the tournament date, the state JC president and his assistant showed up with a photographer. It seemed that the president wanted his picture on the cover of the state JC magazine. We go out to the first tee because he wants the picture to capture him hitting a golf ball. Mr. President tees up a ball and tells the photographer that he will let him know when to take the picture. First he poses himself in a back swing and decides that's no good. Then he tries a variety of follow throughs until he finds just the right one and tells the photographer to go ahead and shoot. The magazine came out about a week before the tournament with a wonderful picture of the president's follow through and the ball still sitting on the tee!

It was in Coffeyville that I learned that there is more to keeping members happy than just smooth greens and praise for their backswing. One day a doctor's wife came to me very upset. She had just had a two-karat diamond reset in a new ring and it had fallen out somewhere on the course. She was offering $100 reward for its return. We scoured the entire course to no avail. It wasn't until we brought in the ball washers for the winter that we found that diamond in the bottom of one of them. I'm sure that she had already made an insurance claim by then, but she was glad to get it back anyway.

Chapter 3

It was in Coffeyville, Kansas that we had an old, 1934 Ford pickup with a full house Mercury engine that had two-foot feeds, one for gas and one for alcohol. At the time Sue didn't know how to drive, so I taught her in the pickup. In the process we wore the rubber completely off the back two tires. We slid through intersections, we skidded to stops all over town, we did doughnuts on Main Street, we went backwards and sideways through stop signs. When Sue finally got the hang of it, I traded the pickup for a 1949 Chevy that a little old lady had owned. Shortly after the trade, I accepted a job in Altus, Oklahoma at the Altus Town and Country Club. We rented a U-Haul trailer, packed up our belongings and hooked the trailer up to the '49 Chevy. It wasn't until this point that I discovered that the little old lady had neglected to put anti-freeze in the radiator and the block was cracked. It had run fairly well until it had to pull the trailer, and then it got hotter than hell. I took it to the local mechanic and he suggested putting a substance called water glass in the radiator to plug up the crack. The engine just sucked every bit of that water glass into the crankcase. When I told the mechanic that I had to go 400 miles to a new job he just laughed and told me that I'd be lucky to make it five miles. I figured that I had to get as close to Altus as I could, since I couldn't afford to buy another car, so we set out down the highway. We stopped at nearly every filling station between Coffeyville and Altus, never once turning off the engine. We pulled into Altus, found our house, which was behind the clubhouse at the course, turned off the engine and that was the last time she ever moved!

In Altus I was a one-man show, there was no help at all. The course consisted of nine holes with grass greens, watered fairways and watered rough. I had one set of mowers, one greens mower and one tractor and they were all antiques. The place was in shambles. It looked for all the world as if it had been deserted. Located in southwestern Oklahoma, the surrounding landscape didn't help the scene any. Arid, very few trees, lots of wind and dust, it's kind of ugly. The only thing that survives there is cotton. The wind blows everyday, every season. There isn't one single day without wind. Everyone around that area leaned a certain way and walked with that side into the wind! When I first arrived I wondered why most of the quick couplers for the sprinklers were way out in the rough. It turns out that they were upwind and the wind blew the water on to the fairway. There are some granite, wind worn hills that break up the scenery, but otherwise there isn't much to see.

The clubhouse was an "L" shaped set of former Air Force barracks which had once been part of Altus Air Force Base, located right next to the course. One of the first members I ran into offered me $350 to burn the clubhouse down. I sure as hell considered it, but I didn't think it was right. Shortly after I left Altus, that old clubhouse burned to the ground. Someone must have made themselves $350.

Not too long after arriving at Altus the club was scheduled to have its' annual championship tournament, the biggest event of the year. A couple of nights before the tournament was to start, I went out to water the greens and found no pressure in the pumphouse. I looked out over the moonlit course and discovered a 100-foot geyser in the middle of the first fairway. It was a mainline water leak. I worked all night and finally got the leak fixed. I came back to the shop about dawn and found the greens mower wouldn't start. It had burned out points. It took about an hour, but I finally got it running and started out to mow the greens. Just as I came out of the barn our greens chairman, who was the local Chrysler dealer, comes roaring up in a big old black Chrysler Imperial. He came to a screeching halt in front of me and jumped out of the car. He said "Why you lazy bastard, are you just now getting out of bed to mow the greens on the biggest day of the year?" I wasn't in the best of moods anyway, so I picked him up and hung him on a railroad spike that was stuck in the side of the barn. I was all set to slap him around when Sue, who had been hanging clothes and witnessed all of this, came running over and made me take him down. Mr. Greens Chairman jumps into his big black Chrysler Imperial and leaves in a cloud of dust. I turned to Sue and told her to start packing, that's the end of this job. I pulled the mower back in the barn and Sue began packing. About an hour later the club president, Jimmy Snell, comes driving up to the house and asks to hear my side of the story. I laid it out for him, blow by blow. When I'm finished, he says that yes, that was the way they heard it and the Board had just finished a brief, ten-minute meeting. They decided unanimously that since, at one time or another, every member of the club had wanted to slap around the Chrysler dealer, they voted me a $100 a month raise. I ran back into the house and told Sue to start unpacking.

Life around a country club is always interesting and filled with unusual characters. One of the most memorable in Altus was an old gentleman who was a fairly wealthy grain elevator owner. He'd show up at the club about once a month with his one eyed Boxer dog. Everybody cringed when the two of them showed up because they both would get stinking drunk at the bar. That old Boxer would sit on a barstool next to the old man and drink Scotch and Sodas right along with him. It got so the members would come in and sit down next to the dog without batting an eye. By the end of the night the dog made as much sense as some of the members! Nobody ever knew which one would pass out first. If the old man passed out first the bartender would continue to give the dog drinks until he passed out, too. At closing time they would just lock the two of them in and the next morning they would be half way sober and the old man would order another round and start all over again. These binges would last for 3 or 4 days and then they would disappear for a month or so before coming back for another binge.

That bar not only provided some pretty interesting characters, it was the setting for some fairly good pranks, too. One cold and blustery day we were sitting watching the 9th green. The wind was blowing out of the north, which is very unusual, and right into the green from the tee. The hole is a long par four, dogleg right with trees in the dogleg. One of the club's better players was out with his wife, who is a rank beginner. As we are sitting there, we see his drive come over the trees and roll across the green. Now I get it in my head that it would be a real good idea if I go out there and put his ball in the hole so he'd think he had a hole-in-one. The rest of the patrons think this would be a wonderful idea. So I sneak out, pick up his ball and put it in the hole before they make it around the trees. I got back in the bar in time to see the two of them come up onto the green and he begins to search for his ball all around the fringe and the rough. He tells his wife to go ahead and putt out while he is searching. Pretty soon she calls out to him that she has his ball. He asked where she had found it. In the hole she says. He comes running into the bar, all excited about his hole-in-one. We were all laughing and grinning at each other until he proclaims that he thinks that it might be a world record hole-in-one and he's going to call the Oklahoma State Golf Association (OSGA) to come out and measure. None of us really wanted to confess, so when the OSGA came out, they found that it was just a few yards short of a world's record! Everyone was sworn to secrecy and to this day that golfer thinks that he made a near world record hole-in-one.

As I said before, I wasn't making big money in those days, so Sue was having to walk to the grocery store, or anywhere else she wanted to go, because that old 1949 Chevy was still sitting in front of our house. Before long we saved enough to put together a down payment on an old clunker. It was a 1952 Chevy Coupe. They agreed to take the '49 Chevy in trade and when they came to pick it up they asked me if it ran. I told them I honestly didn't know, that I hadn't tried to turn it over since we arrived, almost a year before. I can still hear the sound of the tires squealing as they tried to pop the clutch out on the highway.

So now we had transportation and monthly payments that we could just barely afford. We were as poor as Old Job's Turkey. Soon after we made our purchase, Sue got homesick so we decided to go back to Sedan for a visit. We had a nice visit and on the way back we blew out a tire. I pulled over and put the spare on and we continued on. About thirty miles down the road the spare blows out. I just keep driving and Sue asks if I'm going to pull over. I said that I didn't know why I would, we didn't have another spare, so I keep driving and pretty soon the rubber flies off and I'm driving on the rim. That was the left front rim and a few miles later the right back tire blows and it throws rubber all over the highway. Within the next hundred miles the other two tires blow and the rubber has almost beaten the fenders off the car. I'm down to the rims on all four wheels. I just keep on driving because there's nothing else to do. When I would go through towns, it sounded like someone rolling fifty-five gallon drums down the street. Sue was hiding down on the floorboards because she did not want anybody to see her in this contraption. Driving in that car was like driving on ice, but I managed to get pretty good at it and we cruised along about 45 miles an hour, even passing some other cars on the road. We made it all the way home to Altus on those rims, showering sparks on every little town that we passed through. When we got back, I bought four old used tires and put them on those rims and got a lot more mileage out of them. There was a lot of steel in rims in those days.

About the time we are on the verge of falling behind in the payments, I heard about this big money golf game down in Vernon, Texas. I told Sue that we were going to go down there and I was going to make enough money to make a car payment and we'll go eat a T-bone steak. So we drive down to Vernon and I arrive at the course to find three guys on the tee looking for a fourth. When I join them they ask if I'd like to play this game that they always play down there. I figured that I was there for the money, so I said that sure I would. We lagged balls for partners and then they explained the rules to me. We were playing $5 Nassau, automatic press when you're one down, everything pressed on nine, everything pressed on eighteen and fifty-cent birdie eggs, no ties. Now Vernon was a nine hole, grass green course so you played the nine twice in a tournament. We had both been hitting it sideways for seventeen holes. We arrive at the eighteenth hole, which is a par four, dogleg right, uphill to an elevated green. At this exact time the west Texas wind decides to pick up, as it does fairly often in that part of the world. I turned to my partner and told him I thought that we were in pretty bad shape. As near as I can figure it, we're going to lose about $7.50. I was real concerned because I had about $1.50 in my pocket and I was trying to figure out how the hell I was going to pay this off. My partner looked at me kind of funny and asked me if I was kidding. I said no. He said that we stood to lose $800 to $900 at the least. I asked how that was possible and it was then that I learned that we were playing against everyone who had teed off on the golf course since 8:00AM! I'm thinking oh, my God! What am I going to do now? I look beyond the 9th fairway and there's a busy highway real close by. Sue and Rhonda were out in the car in the parking lot doing some sewing. I thought that I might just run out, catch a ride on the highway and try to flag down Sue in the process. So we get up to the green and my partner is laying four and still not on the green. I hit my second shot into a deep trap on the right side of the green. There was nothing to do but say a little prayer and climb down into the bunker. I hit the shot way too hard and it comes out and catches in the flag, hangs there for what seems like an eternity, rolls down the flagstick and into the hole! It turns out that I'm the only one who's birdied the hole all day long. The upshot is that all bets are even and I've got fifty cents coming from everybody! That was the best tasting steak I've ever eaten.

It wasn't long after that that I decided that I had about had it with Altus, Oklahoma. No equipment, no money to do the things that needed doing, there wasn't much to keep us in Altus. I left the Golf Club and we moved into town and I took a job building a practice facility for the Altus

Air Force base. I was working in the alert area, where guys would be stationed for four or five days at a time and be on 24 hour alert. I was building a tee and a green in the space between two runways. They told me that if I ever heard a Bravo Alert over the speakers I was to stay exactly where I was and not move. About two weeks into the project I hear the alert come over the system. B-52s are coming out of one side and KC-135s are coming out of the other side. I was standing next to a huge pile of greensmix, which was sand and peat moss. By the time the last plane was airborne the entire pile was gone. I found most of it in my hair and in my throat and in my nose and in my ears. I dug out sand for a year after that.

While I was building the practice facility, it took the Air Force quite some time to process the paper work and get me my paycheck. Things got pretty tight for a while and we fell behind in our car payments. Also, we were eating nothing but potatoes and drinking water. When the check finally came through, I stopped on the way home and bought two big bags of groceries. I got home and there was a guy from GMAC there to collect the car payments. When I came in Rhonda, our little girl, ripped one bag from my arms and squealed with delight. The GMAC man just nodded at me and left without saying a word. A couple of weeks later another GMAC man showed up and I paid him the back payments and asked where the other fellow was. This guy says he doesn't know but he thinks he quit because he saw just too much grief. One case in particular set him off. It was the site of a starving little girl ripping the groceries out of her daddy's hands that was the last straw.

Since it looked like we were fairly flush for a while, we decided to pay a visit to home, in Sedan. Sue rode the bus and about ten days later I hitchhiked my way back. During that visit I found a job opening in Parsons, Kansas at the Katy Parsons Golf Course owned by the Katy Railroad. To this day I don't know who was the brokest, the railroad or us. Neither of us had any money. We moved everything we owned back to Sedan and stored it in a chicken house.

This course had the first grass greens of any golf course west of the Mississippi. At the time it was built, the Katy Railroad was really flourishing. The railroad would throw what was known as a "Peddler's Party" each year for all of the companies that they did business with. The course was absolutely state of the art at the time. By the time we got there the property was in deep trouble. There were thirty-two members and they told me that if I got the course in really good shape and paid off all of the bills, they would give me what was left over at the end of the year. When all was said and done, there was a little over $900 left at the end of that first year. There was the biggest fight over that $900 you've ever seen! The ladies wanted to paint the Women's Locker Room and the men wanted new ball washers and I never saw a dime of that money. On top of that some members were undercutting me. When I first got there I opened what amounted to a pro shop, selling golf merchandise. This was a first for the Katy Parsons course. There was one board member who got the notion that he would start selling golf merchandise out of the men's locker room. At the next board meeting when it came time for new business, I raised my hand and suggested that this particular board member should be removed from the club for selling merchandise out of the locker room. As you can imagine, there was some spirited discussion after that. Finally the president of the club announces that it is obvious that either the golf pro or the board member would have to go. There were eight members present, including the one in question. The vote was 7-0 in favor of the member leaving, with the member himself abstaining. When the vote was announced, he bolts out of the meeting and disappears. That's when we suddenly realized that we were meeting in his shirt factory. We all quietly left. The next morning Sue is doing the ironing on the screen porch at our house and this same board member pulls up in his big ol' Buick and takes the iron and ironing board right out of her hands. It seems that he had given it to her when we first arrived. It took him about two months, but he did come back and apologized to the board and to Sue and I.

We lived in a house behind the clubhouse that was made out of shell boxes. There was an ordinance plant close by and someone had built this house out of old, wooden shell boxes. It was about ten feet from a rail line and we could look out our window at the trains coming around the curve and see them lean over towards us as if they were going to come right through our kitchen. The trains would straighten back up and go right on by, but I swore to Sue that I was going to find another job before we became casualties. The day did come when one of the boxcars didn't make it around that curve. It didn't hit our house, but it did spill its' load of hogs. Each of the maintenance crew and I picked one up and headed down the road to the local butcher and he slaughtered those hogs for us. I know now what the phrase "living high on the hog" really means! We didn't live up there very often in Parsons believe me. There were times when if it wasn't for some friends by the name of Bill and Ree Wilson, who invited us to dinner from time to time, we may not have eaten! Bill delivered gasoline to me at the course and he really thought that the game of golf was stupid! He made fun of the game and anyone who played it, but he was and is a good friend. Bill and Ree have been our friends for over forty years.

Parsons was the place that I began to learn about organic as opposed to chemical fertilizers. The course just didn't have any money for fertilizers and such, so Sue and I would sneak on to the boxcars behind our house and sweep out the manure left behind from a cattle shipment. We'd put it in gunnysacks and suspend the sacks in 55-gallon drums of water. After about a month or so we had what we called cow manure tea. I used this mixture on the greens and one of the first things that I noticed was that the inch and a half of thatch that had been on the greens was gone. The next thing that I noticed was that virtually everyone who played the course commented on how fantastic the greens were. And they were right. We had the best greens in the country. All because of cow manure tea!

It was there in Parsons that I had an old '37 Chevy pickup that the members called the Deadwood Stage. When this old pickup got up to about twenty-five miles an hour the fenders would flap as if it were trying to fly and as it turned out, it's too bad that it couldn't fly. I had hired this old Hobo off of the tracks to do odd jobs around the course. This guy was an extremely brilliant man, with an engineering degree form Purdue University, who had hit the skids. He acted sort of strange now and then, but he did good work. I let him sleep in the storage room at night. Actually I'd lock him in and let him out in the morning. He'd go get ice in the old pickup truck each morning until the day when he left it parked on the railroad tracks and a train hit it. That was the end of the Deadwood Stage. I got to smelling liquor on his breath and when we did inventory at the end of the month, we found that we were about thirty cases of beer short. We came to find out that he had been drinking the beer and putting the empty cases on the bottom of the stack so it didn't show.

Soon thereafter we were painting the men's and women's locker rooms and we had moved everybody's clubs up to the main part of the clubhouse. It wasn't long before golf balls started disappearing from the members' bags. Now at the time, in addition to the hobo, I had seven young Mexican kids working on the maintenance crew and the members started hollering for me to get rid of the bum and the kids because they just knew it was them that had stolen the golf balls. One day Sue was scrubbing the floor in the clubhouse and was back behind the counter when a board member and his wife come into where the clubs were stored and started going through the bags and stealing golf balls. Sue stayed put and didn't say anything until they left and then she came and told me what had happened. A couple of days later there was a board meeting and the first thing that came up was the question of whether I had fired the kids yet. I locked eyes with the guilty board member and said that no, I hadn't and I wasn't going to because they hadn't stolen any golf balls, but my wife and I knew who did. Of course they wanted to know who it was and I said that I wasn't going to tell them, but I guaranteed them that the stealing was over. Man, that guy was sitting there squirming like a pig under a fence! About a month later there was another board meeting and the president asks if anyone was missing any golf balls that month and everybody shakes their head no and I looked at the offending member and said that there wouldn't be any more missing, either. That member was very uncomfortable, but he never stole another ball and he never said a word to me.

When you are a one-man show at a country club you tend to get wrapped up in a lot of stuff other than golf or greens maintenance. I had ordered some shirts and underwear from Jockey to sell in the pro shop. I came back in from the course one day and there are all of these huge boxes stacked all around the shop. I mean they were huge, four feet tall, three feet wide and as deep. I open them up and they are filled with shirts and underwear. Forty-eight dozen shirts, sixty dozen sets of underwear and forty-eight dozen pairs of socks. Now there is no way that I ordered that many for a little pro shop in Parsons, Kansas. Someone had obviously made a mistake. I figured that I would take care of it the next day. That night we had a gully washer of a rainstorm and water leaked under the roof and ran down a gas pipe and soaked every one of those boxes. Now I'm stuck with several thousand dollars worth of apparel that I would never be able to sell through the shop. I finally found someone to buy the whole lot for twenty-five cents on the dollar. When the last box was finally carted off Sue asked me how many I had kept for myself. She reminded me that I only had three pairs of shorts and they all had holes in them. I hadn't kept one single pair of shorts, socks or shirts! It damn near broke me and I had absolutely nothing to show for the experience! (Click here to input the text of your first chapter or other division.)

Chapter 4

When it came time to move on from Parsons, I took a job in Lyons, Kansas at the Lyons Town and Country Club. Sue was pregnant at the time and just as we got all loaded up and ready to pull out of the driveway, she decides that she's going to have a baby. So instead of driving to Lyons, we head for the hospital. She stays all night and nothing happens. In the morning she decides that she's ok to travel, so we get back on the road to Lyons. When we arrived at the Town and Country Club the members thought that the impending birth was a bigger deal than their new head pro so they started throwing dollar bills into a pot to guess when the baby would arrive. The pot had to be started over four different times because the baby still hadn't been born. Finally, on the 3rd of July our second child, Larry Paul was born. It took so long that it seemed like he was fully grown when he was born! He came out at a hefty nine pounds four ounces.

Lyons, Kansas is located in the western part of the state and is surround by wheat fields, oil wells and silos. Mostly the land is as flat as a pool table. My first week there I was introduced to the President of the bank, Brian Babcock, who was also president of the Board of Directors of the club. The first thing he did was to invite me to take a ride out to see his farm. We hopped into his pickup truck and started down the road. Not too far out of town we turned onto his farm and the banker slammed on his brakes, almost throwing me through the windshield. He reached behind the seat and pulled out a stick of dynamite, got out of the truck and went over to a small boulder on the side of the road. He dug around the base of the rock and set the dynamite in there, lit it, ran back to the truck and we drove down the road like a bat out of hell and then he slammed on the brakes again. We looked back and there was a terrific explosion. I looked over at Mr. Banker and he had a strange grin on his face and he is chortling deep in his throat, sort of "Heh, heh, heh!" I thought to myself, "Oh, man! This is going to be a long year!"

The first job assigned to the new pro at most country clubs is to take care of certain "immediate" problems. I have since learned from first hand knowledge that the "immediate" problems are those which nobody has the guts to take care of! The first job at Lyons was to stop Jim Chew from pinching people. My first question was who is Jim Chew? It turns out that he was the wealthiest man in town, which meant he was the wealthiest member of the club. I asked what they meant by "pinching". They told me that his victims had reported large welts as a result of having been pinched by Jim Chew. They wanted me to put a stop to it! I didn't think much about it until after I had been there about three or four months. One day Jimmy Chew was in the 19th hole and he is pretty well into the sauce and he comes up and pinches me on my biceps and walks away laughing. I went into the men's locker room and rolled up my sleeve and there was the biggest blood blister that I had ever seen! I thought to myself, "Dang! So that's what they're all worked up about!" A few days later I was out in the maintenance shed and I noticed a clamp from a jumper cable hanging on the wall. I immediately knew that it had Jimmy Chew's name written all over it! I took that clamp and stashed it behind the bar. We had a party shortly after that and Jimmy Chew was in rare form. He had already pinched two gals on the butt and one of them came up to me and demanded that I do something about it. I went behind the bar and got out the clamp and went down to where Jimmy Chew is sitting on a barstool. I squeezed that thing open as far as it would go and clamped it on his butt. Now Jimmy Chew was a pretty short and stocky fellow and carried most of his weight in his butt. When that clamp bit down, he jumped up, screaming like a Banshee and running around the bar yelling, "Something's got me! Something's got me!" All the time he is trying to reach behind him to see what, exactly, it is that has him but he can't reach it. He's hollering, "What's got me?" and I walked up to him and pulled the clamp off and show it to him. I told him that I was going to put it behind the bar and the next time that he pinched someone the clamp was going to get him again! That was the last time that Jimmy Chew ever pinched anyone at the club!

Every course has at least one perpetually troublesome green. At Lyons Town and Country Club it was number five. It had a dirt road that went along behind it and two big ol' Cottonwood trees that shaded it. When the greens committee pointed out that they never could keep number five in good playing condition, I told them that it was because the roots of the trees were up into the green and sucking water away from the grass. I said that at least one of those trees had to come down. This caused massive consternation, as it seemed that one of the oldest members had planted those trees and he was still around and playing regularly and no one believed that he would ever allow anyone to take them down. I decided to go and have a talk with the old gentleman. I took him down to number five and showed him the problem and the first thing he says is that we should take out one of those trees, especially the big one in front. I told him that I thought that was a very good idea. The next week I went to the Board of Director's meeting and told them that the member that they were worried about thought that we needed to take out the biggest of the trees. Upon hearing this good news, Brian Babcock, the dynamite toting bank president, jumps up and declares that he will blow it out! My first thought was "Oh, boy, this is going to be a fiasco!"

The next Sunday morning I met Brian and three club members at the tree. He had a trunk full of dynamite and he started to shove sticks under the tree. To this day nobody knows how much he used, but I remember that he made at least five trips back and forth to his car for more. At 5:45AM on that fateful Sunday morning, I touched the wires to the battery on my car and the charge went "KABOOM!" That ol' tree went straight up into the air and settled back down in its' hole and sat there for what seemed like two minutes and then all of the leaves fell off at the same time. I looked across the street and there were people running from their houses, closely followed by huge balls of plaster dust. God Almighty! We ruined at least half a dozen houses! Of course everyone blamed me because I was the one that touched off the explosion. It was about this time that I decided that all bankers were a few bricks shy of a load. I once told a member that the bank in Lyons ought to be padded inside because the president wasn't safe! If that had happened today the lawsuits would have taken twenty years to straighten out. As it was some plasterers got some extra work and folks got a good story to tell for years to come.

It was in Lyons that I met Ralph Terry, the great New York Yankee pitcher. He was married to a gal from those parts and would come by to play golf in the off-season. I lived across the street from the course and one day Ralph pulls up in a brand new Corvette that had been given to him as MVP of the World Series. As I am coming out of the house he tells me to hop in, that he will drive me over to the clubhouse. I get in and he pops the clutch and floors it and we burn rubber all the way to the clubhouse. When we get there, he puts it in reverse and does the same thing back to my house where he throws it in low and floors it back to the clubhouse again. By this time we couldn't see five feet in front of us for all of the smoke. By our fifth round trip every police officer in town is headed our way. Ralph Terry was out there for forty-five minutes signing autographs and not one of them was on a ticket!

All of the smoke and dust finally settled and got cleaned up, but there was a guy named Herb Herble for whom nothing was ever clean enough. He was one of those kinds of guys who would take his handkerchief out to open a door. Immaculate was not an adequate word to describe his habits. Herb had been on the board for a number of years and was very proud to serve. As happens from time to time at most country clubs, the board took on several new members this one year and they voted Herb off of the board. This nearly broke his heart. The next morning, before daylight, I heard all kinds of noise and commotion out on the golf course. I get up and go out there and here is Herb with two oil field crews and he is building a fence right through the seventh green and down the seventh fairway.

I asked him what he was doing and he told me that he owned everything to the left and so half of number seven belonged to him. He says, "If I were you, Runyon, I'd make a few phone calls!" I did just that and all of those new board members came hustling out there. By this time his crews have got the fence almost finished. The board convenes an emergency meeting on the spot and votes Herb back on. Herb was real happy but he says to me, "You know, I think I'll leave that fence up for a week or so, just to teach them boys a lesson!" Where else would something like that happen but at a country club?

The best golfer at Lyons, and a good friend of mine was a guy named Jim Ludes. He was a real gentleman as well as a first class character. The two of us went over to Salina to a big pro-am tournament and we hooked up with touring pro Bo Wininger. Now Bo had been kicked off of the PGA tour for six months because he went on an African safari and missed a couple of tournaments. He wasn't too busy as a result and he asked me what I was doing. I told him that I was trying to raise money to plant trees on the golf course. Bo thinks that planting trees is a pretty nifty idea so he suggests that he come by the club and put on an exhibition to raise some money. Well, Jim Ludes thinks it's a swell idea, too and we start making plans. At the time Jim Colbert was amateur champ of both Kansas and Missouri. Ludes decides that since he is the club champ, he and Colbert will play Bo Wininger and I in an exhibition match. We sold a whole bunch of tickets for this match and a real good crowd showed up. We get the match started and as we get up on the sixth green and I'm lining up my putt, I get handcuffed by a deputy sheriff. It seems that a month before this I had been over in Ellenwood, a neighboring town, playing poker. I left there late at night and drove under a streetlight that was burned out and realized that I didn't have my headlights on. So I flipped on my lights and looked back in my rear view mirror and saw a set of red lights. I figured that I hadn't done anything wrong and I wasn't going to stop since they couldn't be after me. At the time I was driving a big ol' Buick that was just a hell of a car. Just outside of town was an "S" curve and I sort of cut the curves off. I was doing about 120 MPH and didn't think much of it; I had done it before. As I got back on the pavement heading out of town I see the red lights out in the pasture on the right side of the road and then I see them bounce in the ditch on either side of the road and then he comes to a stop in the pasture on the left side of the road. I slowed down enough to see that he hadn't rolled over and he was ok, so I continue on home using the back roads. When I arrive at my house there was a cop from Lyons, whom I knew and he said he only had one thing to ask me; had I been in Ellenwood that day? I said that I had. He said ok, thank you, and left. I didn't think anymore about it until I am lining up that putt on the sixth hole of the exhibition match with Jim Colbert and Bo Wininger and the next thing that I know I am handcuffed. The Deputy had a warrant for my arrest for driving without lights, exceeding 60 MPH in a 40 MPH zone, and exceeding 100 MPH in a 60 MPH zone. Bo is staring in disbelief and asks the Deputy what the hell he thinks he's doing to his partner? I tried to tell the Deputy that if he un-cuffed me I'd take care of the problem after the exhibition. There were about five hundred people at that exhibition, but to this day I don't think Jim Colbert knows that I was handcuffed. He was in the crowd on the other side of the green when all of this happened. Bo Wininger knew, though. He was watching his partner go down the drain! Finally everyone had enough of the joke and they un-cuffed me and the match went on. I did end up paying a hefty fine, but the club got a bunch of new trees out of the episode.

Lyons, Kansas was a one Veterinarian town in those days and his name was Doc Kennedy. If you needed a cow worked on you had to do it by 9:30 AM because by 9:45 Doc was in the sauce. An avid golfer, he had a standing 9:45 tee time every morning. He would come into the pro shop and tell all kinds of stories about cows and their health problems and what he had done for them. I got to feel like a Vet myself. He always called me "onions", I guess partly because he had heard of my ill-fated venture in the onion market and partly because it rhymed with Runyon. One day he came in the shop and says, "Onions, how busy are you?" I said that things were pretty slow that day. He says, "Walt Fillman's old lady bought herself a py-aner and we need some help loading it up." So I called Sue to come and watch the pro shop and while we were waiting for her Doc says that he suspects that the "py-aner" is one of those high backed models that weigh as much as the house. "I believe," he says, "that this job calls for a couple of snifters for fortification before we go." I mixed him up his favorite concoction of Gin and grapefruit juice and as I'm mixing he asks me what I think about the project. The more I thought, the better the idea of a couple of snifters sounded, so I mixed some up for myself. Pretty soon Sue arrived and the good doctor asked, "What do you think about getting some snifters to go?" Well he always carried a Thermos along with him that I would fill up with his favorite drink and that's what I did. When we got to the place where the piano was we discover that, sure enough, it was one of those old, high backed Honky Tonk pianos that weigh a ton. We somehow managed to muscle the thing down to the pickup truck and get it loaded. After a toast to our success, we head off down the road to Walt Fillman's old lady's house. About half way there, Doc looks back and says, "By God, son, the py-aner is gone!" I looked back and sure enough, there is no trace of the py-aner! I turned the truck around and headed back down the road and about eight miles back we found Mrs. Fillman's py-aner. It was scattered on both sides of the highway and all across the road. Traffic was slowing down to avoid the pieces, the biggest of which was the keyboard. We get out of the truck to survey the scene and Doc says, "Onions, she's played her last tune!"

Several years later, when we moved to De Kalb, Illinois, Sue was listening to the radio and heard this lady offer a free piano to anyone who would pick up and deliver her new one and pick up her old one. Sue was the first one to call and when I got home she told me that she had found Rhonda a piano. My first thought was "Oh, God, I'll bet it's an old fashioned, high backed py-aner! "And," I told Sue, "I bet it's on the second floor, too." Well I had only been in De Kalb for three or four days and didn't really know anybody well enough to ask them to help me. I spotted a bum walking down the street and asked him if he'd like to earn some money by helping me move a piano. He said that sounded fine and off we went. When we got there the first thing I noticed was that the house was built on the side of a hill and there were, by actual count, forty seven steps leading up to it. When we got inside I found that it was almost a twin of Mrs. Fillman's ill-fated py-aner! The bum and I scratched our heads and tried to figure out how in the world we were going to get that py-aner down forty-seven steps. The first thing to do, we ascertained, was to get it out of the house and on to the front porch. Well, guess what? We never had to worry about the steps because when we pushed that thing out onto the porch it went right through it and landed two stories down under the house! It made such a hell of a noise that I couldn't hear for three days! The bum said that he only had one good ear and it was gone forever. We went down to look at it and found that it wasn't in too bad shape, but it took me two days to glue all of the pieces that had fallen off. When we delivered it to the lady she hit a few keys and the only sound was a very dissatisfactory "Thunk". She said she'd have to have a piano tuner out to tune it. I picked up the piano that she was giving us and hauled it home. We were living in a two-story house at the time and don't you know that it had to go upstairs! We got it up there and Rhonda started her lessons. I think she took all of three lessons before she quit. The piano sat there gathering dust until we sold the house and I left it behind for the new owners.

After the Lyons incident some of my friends put an ad in the paper for piano moving and my phone number in it. I got all kinds of calls and I told them that I had gone out of business. After word got around in De Kalb and I told a few people the story of Doc and the py-aner, a similar ad appeared in the De Kalb paper, again with my phone number.

In those days most country clubs had slot machines in the bar area. They were illegal, but it was something that was just done anyway. We had a false front wall that we could slide a panel back and hide the slots. We'd get a call that the authorities were coming out and we should put the slots away for a couple of days. Now these machines were heavy, well over a hundred pounds, and of course bulky. They weren't something that could casually be put away. One day we get a panic phone call saying that there is a surprise raid coming our way, no warning. I got two of the three slots behind the wall and I've got the third about half way to the wall when the cops walk in. They make me take it down to the local scrap yard and beat it to pieces with a sledgehammer. It seemed like most of the townsfolk were out there and they were sure that I was going to hell in a handcart since I look like a convict on the chain gang beating rocks!

It was while I was at Lyons that I bought myself an airplane. It was a neat little J-3 Cub and I used the eighth fairway as my landing strip and I parked it behind the maintenance shed. I took Mondays off in those days and I'd go out early and take off and fly around the countryside. I kept that plane there for at least a year. Everyone thought that was kind of unique. One day our bartender, Susan, who was Herb Herbal's daughter (he was the guy who built the fence down the seventh fairway), brought in the first hippie that I had ever seen. This was the early 60's remember, there weren't too many of them yet. So Susan tells me that this guy has never been up in an airplane and would I give him a ride? I said sure, why not? So we take off in my J-3, which had tandem seating, and gain some altitude and I look back to see how he's doing. He points to his stomach and says he wants me to buzz him right there. He's looking for a thrill. I climb to get some altitude and do a hammerhead stall. I leveled out and looked back to see how he's doing and he's out colder than a cucumber and he's got blood running over the top of his left ear. I haven't got a clue as to what is wrong with him, but I figure I'd better get him on the ground pretty quick. So I come around and land and he starts to come around. I get out and go to see if he's ok and I notice that he is holding a ball-peened hammer that I had left behind the rear seat when I had changed a flat tire. He says "Hey, man, you buzzed me right here!" and he points to his head! It was a hell of a thing to do to guy on his first airplane ride.

This was about the time that Arnold Palmer and Jack Nicklaus were coming into prominence and golf was booming. We heard about an exhibition that the two of them were putting on and we went down to the Prairie Dunes Country Club in Hutchinson, Kansas to see it. I saw something there that I had never seen before and never expect to see again. Palmer was on the right hand side of the practice range and Nicklaus was on the left hand side. They were shooting at the same target out on the range and their balls would cross in flight. Not too many shots into the practice their two balls collided in mid-air! Palmer immediately holds up his hand and says, "No, no, don't ask us to do it again. We only do that once per exhibition!" You'd be surprised how many people in the crowd were convinced that they had done it on purpose!

Chapter 5

When it came time to move on from Lyons to Fort Riley, Kansas, the membership threw us a big going away party. It started out at the country club and ended up much later that night at Herb Herbal's beach house at one of the local lakes. Susan, our bartender, had invited all of these college students up from Kansas State for the party. Sometime in the wee small hours of the morning she asks the crowd, "How many want to go skinny dipping?" Everybody raises their hands except my wife, Sue. It was then that I noticed that I had my hand higher than anybody's. One look at Sue and I brought mine down. The whole crowd takes off for the lake and they hadn't been gone more than ten minutes when I tell Sue that I've got an 8:00AM appointment with the Commanding General of the 1st Infantry Division the next morning and I've got this little drive between here and there and I think I really need a little dip to refresh me. Sue allows that this isn't a bad idea, but she's going down there with me. We get down to the end of the dock and I take all of my clothes off and take a look around. It's a beautiful moonlit night and I could see the others out a ways in the lake. I poise myself on the dock and ready myself for a picture perfect dive. I had done a lot of diving as a kid, off high dive towers and bridges. I was pretty good, too. It's about fifteen feet from the dock to the surface of the lake since the water level was down somewhat. I dive off that dock and discover that the water isn't deep enough to cover a Coke bottle! I find myself face down in the mud bottom, knowing I'm alive but thinking I'm going to die and hoping it'll be soon. I had knocked all of the wind out of me and I'm laying in the water for a while, listening to the rest of the party down the shore a ways giggling and carrying on. Pretty soon Sue, who is standing back on the dock and hadn't seen me land, says, "Larry you get your ass back up here!" I finally regained the use of some fingers on my left hand and have managed to gasp some air and Sue hears me. She calls out, "Is that you? Have you swum down there and back?" She thought that I had swum down to the crowd and had some fun. I climbed back up on the dock and we get me cleaned up and discover that I don't have any skin left on my forehead, my chin, the back of my hands, the back of my forearms or my knees.

At precisely 8:00AM the next morning I'm standing before the Commanding General of Fort Riley. He takes one look at me and says, "Good God Almighty! What happened to you?" When I opened my mouth to try and tell him I started bleeding! My first day on the job was spent mostly in sickbay getting patched up.

I was at Fort Riley for almost five years and was the Pro Superintendent of two courses; the officers only course and the enlisted man's course. I had the bar and the pro shop at the officer's course and the outside maintenance for both courses. The bar at the officer's course was the only bar on the post that was allowed to open before 4:30 in the afternoon and I opened mine at 7:00AM. There was a line waiting for opening time every morning!

When we first arrived in town we moved into a nice little house in a nice neighborhood and for the first three days we were there we had a parade of people knocking at the door. A parade of men of all ages and descriptions. They were actually looking for the house next door. It was then that we learned that we were living next to a whorehouse! Well, Sue wasn't overly thrilled with this situation, especially when most of the men would eye her up and down and think that they had hit the jackpot! We stayed in that house the shortest amount of time that we could and then moved into a house owned by one of the local bankers. We were there for thirty days and he sold it. Now we've got to move again. We found a house that was owned by a preacher who each and every first of the month was on our doorstep at the crack of dawn looking for his rent money. We didn't even have a chance to eat breakfast before he was knocking at the door. From there we moved into a house where a Second Lieutenant and his young bride were living in the basement and we were living upstairs. That was quite an entertaining place to live. There was a vent that came from the basement, past our bed and up to the roof. Every word that either of them uttered was magnified and piped into our bedroom. There were some fairly entertaining moments, but it got so we had a hard time getting any rest! I finally went down and knocked on their door and told the Lieutenant that if he didn't quit practicing this march that he was on, I was never going to get any sleep. He was a bit bewildered until I told him that we could hear every word that he and/or his wife even whispered! I'm sure that they were happy when we moved shortly thereafter.

When I first started at Fort Riley I was working for a General Seaman. This General really loved trees. They were a passion of his. At the same time there was a Major who used to come into the pro shop every afternoon and ask to see a Titleist golf ball. I'd hand it to him and he would roll it around in the palm of his hand, hand it back to me and tell me that he was going to buy one of them some day. Finally the big day came and he actually bought one. He went out to play his round and some time later he came back in and asked me if I had a saw. It seems that he had wedged his brand new Titleist in the crotch of a tree and just couldn't get it out. He showed me the grip on his seven iron that was all chewed up and mangled where he had tried to get that ball out. He wanted to saw the branch off. I told him that he had better kiss that Titleist goodbye. The next morning at dawn I drove into the golf course and I find the Major and three Privates walking in from the course. The Major holds his Titleist up and proclaims that he has retrieved it from the tree. I asked him how he managed that. His group had cut down the tree! I couldn't believe my eyes. There was the tree, lying across the dogleg on number seven. I told him that I could end his career right on the spot if I had a mind to. I told him of the General's passion for trees. I told him to get the mess on number seven cleaned up and then I would decide whether or not I was going to turn him in. Luckily there was a clump of trees there at the dog leg and the absence of one didn't show up that much so I never turned him in, but he was the most fanatical Titleist owner that I ever met!

Another strange tale concerning golf balls had to do with the wife of a full Colonel. She would come in to buy a new ball every time she'd play. She'd take it out and play number one and number two and then most times she would come back to the pro shop and want to trade in her ball because it didn't work right! I had instructions from her husband to keep track and he would come in once a month to settle up with me. If she got through the first two holes in par or one over, then it was a good ball, if not, in she'd come for a new one. That lasted for about two years until they got transferred out.

Another Colonel came into the pro shop one day when Sue was behind the counter. She noticed that he had left one of the pockets on his golfbag open and was losing golfballs as he walked. Sue called out to him, "Colonel, sir, your zipper is open and your balls are falling out." He immediately dropped his bag and reached for the zipper on his pants. "Oh, no, sir, your GOLF balls!" He had a good laugh and he never let Sue forget it!

About this time I went over to Wichita, Kansas to play in a pro/am tournament. I didn't take any amateurs with me because they said that they would give me an A, B and C player. When I got there I found out that I had two C players and a D minus player who had only been playing golf for six weeks. For the first two days we did nothing but look for his ball. Every time Mr. D Minus would tee it up we would all look in a different direction. He kept saying that by gosh he was going to help our team. On the third day we were actually doing pretty well. We came to an elevated par three with a creek that ran in front of the green and along the right side. We all hit in the creek except Mr. D Minus who knocked it on the green, six feet above the hole. On the way to the green he says, "I told you boys I'd help this team!" We got to the green and the three of us pick up or balls and put them in our pockets. Our hero gets settled over this six-foot putt and he freezes. He looks like a statue standing there! Soon there were two foursomes backed up behind us and I suggested that he back off from the putt and take a deep breath. He allows as that might be a good idea and takes a little walk around the green, huffing and puffing. He finally settles in over the putt again and again turns into a statue! Quincy Utter finally just couldn't stand it any longer and yells, "Hit it!" The guy knocked it in the creek! We ended up taking a nine on the hole.

That same tournament was where we complained about slow play almost constantly. I was the biggest complainer of all. As I sat on a tee waiting for the fairway to clear so we could tee off, I look up on the hill and saw Wesley Hospital where I had gone through years of treatment for my polio. I got to thinking "My gosh. Here I am complaining about slow play, playing golf as a professional and I've forgotten about all of those years that I hung around that hospital." After we got through with the round I went out and bought a bunch of candy and went up to the fifth floor of the Wesley Hospital, where all the kids hung out, and spent the rest of the afternoon passing out candy. I don't think I've complained about slow play since.

There was another Pro/Am at Rolling Hills Country Club in Wichita one year. The situation was similar; the tournament assigned me three amateurs to play with. I arrived in town on a Sunday night for a Monday tournament. At that time Kansas is absolutely dry. A drink could not be legally consumed anywhere. I managed to find out about a place downtown, located in a basement, that had a one armed piano player and a buxom blonde dancing on top of the piano. They also served adult beverages. I enjoyed myself and stumbled into my room at the Holiday Inn about 5 in the morning. I figured that I had a 9:30 AM tee time, so I could grab a couple hours sleep and make it no sweat. I woke up, looked at the clock and it said 6:30. I figured that I still had a little time so I rolled over and went back to sleep. The next time I rolled over the clock read 9:15. I thought "Good God! I've got a 9:30 tee time!" I jumped into my clothes, didn't shower or shave or anything, drove like a bat out of hell to the course, thinking we are going to be disqualified before we ever swing a club. As I drove into the course I thought to myself "Self, this tournament is sure going to hell, they're letting women play in it!" There were women everywhere! On the tees, in the clubhouse, on the range, everywhere! That's when I discovered that I was exactly one day and 15 minutes late! I had slept for 24 hours. It was Tuesday...ladies day! When I looked at the clock at 6:30 it was 6:30 Monday night!

As I said before, the General was passionate about trees and he decided to sponsor this big Arbor Day. He came by the pro shop one day and asked me how many trees would I like to be planted on the golf course? I asked him how many could I have? He said I could have as many as I liked. I thought that this sounded pretty good so I asked what I had to do? He said that I should go out and put a stake wherever I wanted a tree and keep count so that when Lieutenant Labinski called I could give him the number that I wanted. Sure enough, about three days later Lt. Labinski called and asked in a slow, southern drawl, how many markers did I have laid out? I told him that there were one hundred and eighty seven stakes marking tree locations. He said that he would be down the next day to make all of the necessary preparations. As promised, the next day he shows up with twenty-eight privates, each armed with either a shovel or a pick. Bringing up the rear was a duce and a half water truck. At this point the Lieutenant asks me how deep I thought the holes should be. I told him it depended upon how big the trees were. "Oh, these here are fairly nice sized trees, Sir." He says. In that case, I told him they should be about this deep and this big around, holding out my hands about two and a half feet apart. So the troops proceed to dig all one hundred and eighty seven holes and we get back to the pro shop and the good lieutenant starts to wondering where the trees are, since they should be delivered about then. One of the privates pipes up and says that he has the trees, so the lieutenant calls his troops together for tree unloading detail. "Where are these trees, private?" "Right here, sir." The private hands him a bundle wrapped in brown Kraft paper and tied with string. Inside were one hundred and eighty seven seedling trees each of which was no bigger that a number two pencil. Undaunted, Lieutenant Labinski had his men go ahead and plant each and every tree, one in each two and a half foot wide, two and a half foot deep hole. I went back there some twenty years later and I think each and every one of those trees survived! You just can't beat a well-prepared hole for planting!

It was at Fort Riley that I bought a Rolls Royce. A 1935 Rolls Royce to be precise. It was a beauty. It had a yellow and black paint job, a bar and two vases for fresh roses each day. My bartender, Dooley, doubled as chauffeur. I bought it in Anaheim, California and drove it to Fort Riley. Along the way I discovered that the car had some engine problems, so when I got it home I decided that it would make the classiest watering truck in the history of golf maintenance. We didn't have in-ground irrigation so all watering had to be done with hoses and at night. In those days I would open the course at 6AM and get through with the watering about 1AM. I'd drive that Rolls Royce from hole to hole, moving the hoses and sprinklers.

One night I was well into the watering and I had pulled up next to the sixth green and I could see flashing red lights approaching at a pretty good clip. I pulled over and turned out the lights and started towards the green to turn off the water. The approaching car was the base MP's and they were going so fast that when they slammed on the brakes they skidded to a stop right in the middle of the green! They got out and demanded to see my ID so I showed them my driver's license. They wanted a military ID and I told them that I was a civilian and worked there. "Besides," I said, "You better show me your ID's because when the greens chairman, who just happens to be your boss, sees what you've done here, I'm sure you'll have a very interesting conversation!" It took some doing to get that patrol car off that green because the longer they talked, the deeper it sank into that wet green. I could hear the water bubbling up around the tires. I don't believe that I ever saw those two MP's around the fort after that. Unfortunately my watering truck didn't last long after that, either. As I said, it had engine problems and I ended up selling it to a lawyer in Topeka, Kansas who could afford to fix it up.

There came a time at Fort Riley when the First Division moved out, literally over night. The next day the base was empty. The plan was to build up the Ninth Division from scratch, but that took some time. There was a picture in the Army Times of me with the caption that read, "Golf Pro has his own two private golf courses". Finally a general by the name of Eckhart arrived on post and I got permission to allow civilians to come in to play until the Ninth Division got built up. I figured that the best way to let people know would be to have a golf party. I put together a tournament and invited folks from all of the surrounding towns to come and play. There was just a ton of people that showed up and they all stayed at the bar afterwards. About 10PM that night some of them got to talking about the third hole and how difficult it was. It was a par three and it was tough because there was a cross wind that blew across the fairway that you couldn't feel on the tee. I told them that I could go out in the dark and put one out of two shots on that green and I had twenty dollars that said so. Man, there was some quick action on that! Pretty soon there was over $600 on the table and we were headed out to the third tee, which was right in front of the bar. All assembled allowed that I could use my pickup truck's lights to tee the ball up, so I did. About two thirds of the way trough my first swing, Sue says, "Larry, there goes your pickup!" It backed off the tee, turned itself around and headed down number two fairway. Down at the end of the fairway was the busiest road on the Post. I could see all of the lights of the trucks and jeeps and other traffic going back and forth. A good friend of ours, Ron Freem, chased down the pickup, jumped up on the running board and just as he was about to climb in, the truck hit a bunker and threw him off. It kept going towards a grove of trees that I thought would stop it for sure. It missed every tree in the grove and kept on going. It had clear sailing to the road about this time and I couldn't even watch. Man, this was going to be something Godawful! It hits a storm drain down in a ditch, bounces straight up in the air and bangs around in the ditch and finally there it sits. We get down there and find that the truck has a bent up bumper and some scratches, but otherwise is fine. We drive it back up to the third tee and set up to resume the bet. Six of the guys go down and stand on the green to verify where the ball goes. The very first ball that I hit bounces off of Kite Thomas's foot and goes into the hole for a hole-in-one! I turned to the assembled onlookers and said, "See, I told you this wasn't a very hard hole!" That story appeared in the local papers and got picked up on the AP wire and appeared all over the country.

Fort Riley had a lot of history connected to it. One of the little known facts is that it was the center of the hemp growing industry during WWII. The majority of the rope that the Army used in the war was made from hemp that was grown on the base. As a result, some of the finest marijuana in the country flourished almost everywhere that you looked. During one rainy season we developed a leak in the roof of the pro shop and it got pretty persistent. I kept meaning to call the base engineers to come and fix it but I always seemed to be too busy. One day Sue mentions that our young assistant pro, Gary, was trying to fix the leak but he wasn't having much luck. I didn't know anything about it, but Sue said she had seen him climb up on the roof several times. I went and got a ladder and climbed up there and I almost fell off when I saw what looked to be about $100,000 worth of marijuana drying on my roof! It disappeared after I pointed out to Gary that neither one of us would live long enough to finish our jail time if anyone saw his stash drying out. Luckily the engineers didn't show up until Gary got it all down.

One of the things that I've always enjoyed most about being a head golf pro is that there are so many facets to the job and each one has its own reward. The teaching aspect of the job was always interesting, but it got especially so in the weeks leading up to a tournament, particularly a women's tournament. It's like cramming for a test the night before finals; everyone thinks that they will fine-tune their game with a few lessons. This one time before a big women's tournament, this gal came to me for lessons and I could see right off what her problem was. She put Dolly Parton to shame. She had a pretty good practice swing, but when I put a ball down she had a heck of a time hitting it. She finally asked me if she was supposed to swing over or under. Since there was not one blessed thing that I could do about her problem I told her that as far as I was concerned she could stand there all day and swing any way she wanted! I realize how sexest that sounds today but shoot, I'm only human!

Finally the big annual women's tournament rolled around. Women from the entire surrounding region were invited to play. Along with the golf they had a wine tasting after they played. Now one of the things that I have learned during my time as a pro is that it never pays to interfere with women. Even when you know that they are making mistakes, it is best to just let them go and hope for the best. At this particular event they had the prizes set up on four tables and nobody was monitoring the prizes. They started with "D" flight and worked their way up. Well don't you know that the "D" flight ladies came up and took the nicest prizes, cherry picking the two tables. By the time that the "A" flight championship golfers got up there the only prizes left were the last place hardware. A fistfight broke out between a "D" flight lady and an "A" flight lady. They were really going after each other and when I jumped in between them, they both turned on me! They said, "You burr headed bastard, it's all your fault!" To this day I'm not sure what hit me, but I got two black eyes in ten minutes. I did learn a hard lesson, though. If you ever get involved with women in any activity that involves prizes or rules, unless you are equipped with full football or riot gear, leave them alone!

Another aspect of being the head pro is the supervising of the upgrading of course facilities. We had built a new driving range and clubhouse and everyone was real proud of it. We decided to have an exhibition to commemorate the opening. We invited the local pros and some Kansas City pros to come down and play. We also invited Bob Stone who was a tour player at the time, Joe Jimenez who went on to win the PGA Senior Open and Lou Kretlow who had the world's longest hole-in-one at the time. The idea was for Kretlow to hit the driver, Stone to hit the four wood and Jimenez to hit the short irons. It was a great idea, but Lou Kretlow duck hooked 200 balls. He just couldn't do anything right. He tried everything, but the more he tried, the worse it got. He never got one drive off of the ground. Finally it started raining and everyone made a bee-line for the brand new clubhouse. Now we've got the Army Band there and a whole lot of Army brass as well as our invitees. They all ran into the brand new clubhouse. It was after we all got inside that we discovered that the brand new roof on the brand new clubhouse leaked! We passed out every umbrella that we had in the pro shop and everyone opened them up in the clubhouse. Some of the guys figured they would be better off outside and weathered the storm out there.

Being head pro does present some interesting opportunities, especially on an Army Post. I had always wanted to see one of the "Honest John" missiles fired off. These were the missiles that they used in Korea. These things were fifty-five feet long, capable of carrying a nuclear warhead and were launched from a two and a half ton truck. I kept asking a Captain Mullin, who was in charge of the unit, if I could watch one being fired off. He told me it was impossible, since they were Top Secret. Finally one day he stuck his head in the door of the pro shop and asked if I'd like to be at a VIP firing the next morning at 9AM up on the rimrock. He said coat and tie were the uniform of the day for civilians. So I got up bright and early the next morning, put on my brand new Kuppenhimer suit and brand new necktie and headed for the site. It had rained the night before and it was pretty muddy up there, but they had some bleachers set up for us dignitaries. I climbed up on the stands and looked out at this big old rocket sitting out there poised to launch on its truck. Captain Mullin announced that they were ready for the firing and they did a count down and pushed the button. The rocket took off with a mighty roar and started down range. The only blot on an otherwise perfect launch was the fact that the truck went right along with the rocket! We were all sitting there watching intently and I'm thinking to myself that I don't think that the truck is supposed to go along for the ride! As we watch, the rocket and truck are bumping along the ground and about a quarter of a mile or so out, the two of them turn around and head back towards the reviewing stands. Everybody starts bailing out and heading below the rimrock, which is so sharp that it shreds my brand new Kuppenhimer suit. It was so bad that when I got home, Sue just threw it in the trash. I never did see Captain Mullin after that. I don't know where he got shipped to, but it must have been somewhere worse than Fort Riley, Kansas!

Fort Riley was just one adventure after another. One early morning a maintenance worker named Shump and I were out changing cups on the greens, getting ready for the day's play. I walked up onto the eighth green, which was a very high, elevated green and here was this guy laying face down, arms stretched out. I approached him and saw a bullet hole in the back of his head. I called the MPs and they showed up along with the Highway Patrol. It turned out that the Highway Patrol had been chasing a car with three guys in it the night before and the guys bailed out of the car right at the golf course and ran across the 8th green. One of the officers fired a warning shot in the air and apparently didn't fire high enough and hit the guy in the back of the head! Since the officer was down in a depression and the guy was way up on the green, the officer thought that he was firing well over their heads. Old Shump looked on for a while and then went ahead and moved the cup so people could go ahead and play through! No sense in spoiling a good day for golf!

During this time I was still trying to payoff my losses from the Jockey underwear fiasco in Parsons. As a result, I didn't quite have enough money to stock the pro shop in Fort Riley. It was then that I met up with Ron Fogler, the future Vice President of the PGA and a partner of Jim Colbert's. He helped Sue and I get back on our feet and helped stock the pro shop. Sue and I remain grateful for his help. I also was doing a lot of teaching at the time and I had so many lessons scheduled that it was driving me nuts, so I raised my fee. I got more Lessons. I raised my fee again.

More lessons. After the third time I quit raising the fee, I didn't have anymore time!

One of my lessons was a full Colonel and one day he told me to cancel all of my lessons for the next day, that he was bringing something Top Secret down to the driving range and he wanted me to give him a lesson. The next morning a big Army truck shows up and a three-man crew gets out and starts setting up equipment under this big tree where I gave lessons. It turns out that it was closed circuit television. They hung the camera up on the limb of that tree and started taping. It was my first experience with videotape and it was the first time that I had ever seen a golf swing from the top. I realized right then and there that I had been teaching the wrong moves. For years thereafter I called it "Golfing from the top". It turned out to be the modern golf swing, utilizing the bigger muscles and a big rotation.

Just before I left Fort Riley Dick Musial, Stan Musial's son, was stationed at the fort. He and his wife, Sharon, had just had a baby. One day Dick came to me and said that his dad was coming to town to see them and his new grandchild. This was at the time that Stan the Man was retiring from the St. Louis Cardinals. Dick said that he hadn't told anyone that his dad was coming and that he would like me to set up a golf game for the next morning for he, his dad, myself and one other player. He said that he wanted to spend some time with his father without crowds of his fans around. I recruited my greens chairman, Major Scott, to fill out the foursome. We teed off, and when we got to the ninth tee I had been watching Stan swing and I asked him if he minded some advice. He said he would be glad to listen. I told him that he didn't have the prettiest swing that I had ever seen, but I wanted him to tee one up and pretend he was hitting a home run. Stan Musial hit that golf ball farther than I had ever seen one hit before. The one thing I learned from him that day is that he used his body. The prevailing wisdom among golf teachers at that time was all hands and rotation. Musial's swing was one of the first full body swings that I had ever seen. We played a very pleasant round and went back to the bar for a couple of drinks before the Musials left. Several weeks later Dick walked into the pro shop and told me, with tears in his eyes, that the round of golf was the first time in his life that he had been able to spend a whole day alone with his dad without anyone interfering.

Chapter 6

It was at Fort Riley, Kansas that I decided that I really didn't want the hassle of running and merchandising the pro shop in addition to my other duties. I got to look around and landed a job as just a golf course superintendent in De Kalb, Illinois. My first day on the job was the day before Thanksgiving and was almost my last! It was an abnormally warm day, in the 60s, and I decided to play a round of golf on this new course of mine. When I got through and was putting my clubs in the car, the Greens Chairman comes up to me and asks me what I thought I was doing? I told him that I had just finished a round of golf. He told me that I couldn't play there. I asked what he meant. He said that Superintendents weren't allowed to play on the course. I informed him that he could take his job as Golf Course Superintendent and shove into an orifice that would make it impossible for him to sit down for a very long time! The controversy that ensued was such a brouhaha that the Board of Directors finally voted me a full membership which meant that I had full voting privileges. It turns out that my Greens Chairman was a corporate member and didn't have any voting privileges. That cut him deeply. We had a real interesting relationship after that.

My one concession to that Greens Chairman was to move the fairway bunker on the number five fairway from the right side to the left side. You see, he had a bad slice and would invariably end up in that trap. The next year saw a new Greens Chairman who was a hooker so we moved the trap back to the right hand side. Don't ever let anyone tell you that country clubs aren't about politics.

Whenever I think of De Kalb, Illinois I think of two things; the birth of my second daughter, Robin, and corn. The landscape was gently rolling farmland and almost every available acre was planted in corn. It always amazed me that you could see corn all the way to downtown Chicago from the cornfields of De Kalb. Some of the best farmland in the world butts up against the Chicago city limits!

A side benefit of the job at DeKalb was the proximity of Dick's Ten-0-Nine Tavern. It was a great Irish pub where all of the golfers hung out. Dick O'Donnell was the owner and he and all of his brothers took their Irish heritage seriously. I found out how seriously one St. Patrick's Day when I went in to get some corned beef and cabbage and a few beers. Now I knew very little at that time about Irish history. I have learned a great deal since, but that particular day I walked in wearing an orange, Alpaca sweater! Now in case you don't know, there are two colors that the Irish have very strong feelings about. The predominately Catholic Republic of Ireland has a fondness for Green, while the British ruled Northern Ireland favors orange. The Orange Lodges of the north are very much protestant and anti-Catholic. Wearing orange into an Irish/Catholic bar on St. Patrick's Day is akin to waving a red cape at a bull! I had absolutely no idea that orange was a no-no. I no more than set foot in the bar than I found myself sitting in the middle of the street, 86'd by Dick and his brothers! Chagrinned, I went home and had a very quiet St. Patrick's Day. The next morning I got a phone call from Dick O'Donnell. He told me that if I ever wanted to enter the Ten-O-Nine Tavern and be in the patron's good graces again, I had to bring the offending orange wear down by 10:30 that morning and they were going to burn the clothes in the middle of the street! I asked Sue if she had any old clothes that weren't worth anything that were orange. She gave me an old orange sweatshirt and I hurried down to Dick's. When Dick saw the sweatshirt he just shook his head. "That's not what you were wearing! You had on a bright orange Alpaca sweater." I asked if he knew how much Alpaca sweaters sold for. He said it didn't make any difference to him, but if I ever wanted to be in the good graces of the tavern and the Irish, I had to bring the exact article of clothing. "And," he said, "You've only got one hour to do it!" I went home and told Sue what I was doing and she thought I was crazy. She may be right, but I raced back down to the Ten-O-Nine Tavern and handed my Alpaca sweater to Dick and his brothers. They had a big crowd of patrons gathered around and I'll be damned if they didn't burn that Alpaca sweater right there in the middle of the street!

It's funny how things seem to even out in life. The next Halloween, after the Alpaca burning incident, I told Dick about a prank that I used to pull on Halloween. I'd put on a rubber mask and wrap a sheet around me and when I got on the porch I'd kneel down and stick a pair of little kid's shoes out from under the sheet. When the candy was offered I'd stick out my big ol', hairy hand. Folks got real excited at that. Now Dick thought that was a swell idea and he knew just the folk to pull it on. "Let's go to my brothers' houses and Trick or Treat for drinks!" We recruited Joe Hoynes to get us set up on the porch and ring the bell. We started at Dick's youngest brother. We kneeled down to look like kids and Joe rang the doorbell and out comes Ed O'Donnell with a big smile and a huge bowl of candy. Just as he opens the door Dick sticks his hand out and we both jump up. Ed screams "Ahhhhh" and throws the bowl of candy over his head. I don't know who was more shook up, Ed or the two of us! So we had our shot and then we all went to the rest of Dick's brothers' houses, getting a shot at each one. Finally we end up at Cletus's house and he decides that it would be a good idea to go to the home of a friend of theirs from the bar. So we do and we all start to get set up on the porch. I didn't know this guy, and what we all didn't know was that some Halloweeners in that area had molested this guy earlier in the evening. As we are getting set, the guy looks out of his window and sees the commotion and goes out the side door and comes up behind us with a baseball bat. He spots our big shoes coming out the back of our sheets and starts swinging at Dick. He is just beating him something awful. I rip my mask off and of course he doesn't know me from Adam so he takes another swipe at Dick. The brothers finally convince the guy that they are friends and he quits hammering Dick. The next morning I went in to see how Dick was doing. I saw him behind the bar with two black eyes, knots all over his head and a fat lip. The first thing that he said was "OUT! Get out of here right now! I don't even want to talk to you, Runyon! You're liable to have another idea and I don't want to fall for it. The hell with you. Get the hell out of here. I'm half dead!" He acted as if it were my fault!

In those days most country clubs were pretty thin on funds and a smart superintendent had to come up with some rather innovative methods of fundraising. I had hired this big ol' lumberjack from Wisconsin and he and I were talking about how thin the budget was and how badly we needed some new equipment. He came to me one day and says that he had just completed a survey of the trees on the course and he found that we had 378 trees that were big enough to tap for sap and we could make maple syrup. I said that I didn't know anything about making maple syrup. He reminds me that he is from Wisconsin and that was all that he was doing for the past few years. He knew all of the techniques and formulas. I asked if we could make any money doing this and he gave me the reasonable answer of "It depends upon how much we charge for it!" We decided to make up a small batch and see how it went. We went out to the nearest maple tree and drilled a hole in the trunk. Using an airification spoon from a Ryan airifier we tapped the tree and hung a bucket and waited. We ended up with fifteen gallons of what was referred to as water which we took into the maintenance shack and boiled down to syrup. Those fifteen gallons made about a quart of syrup. I had never tasted real, honest to God maple syrup before. I thought that I had died and gone to heaven! I learned that we could cut that syrup about 25 to 1 and still have the best tasting syrup anywhere. I went to the board of directors and told them my plan to finance next year's budget and they were, to say the least, skeptical. Several of them uttered "Bullshit" out loud. I pulled out my first quarts that I just happened to have brought along. I had a jar for each of the directors. I asked them to taste their sample. I got a unanimous vote to proceed with the maple tree tapping. That first year we sold a jar for $8.00

and completely sold out. During the next four years we got so that there was a waiting list for our syrup.

Any good golf superintendent at a small club will tell you that he has to constantly be on the lookout for money saving and/or making opportunities. In addition to our maple syrup venture, I came up with an idea to take advantage of the wintertime and the snow that usually covered the course. At the time, snowmobiles were just getting started and were a novelty. One of our members, who owned an S&L in town, was also one of the first Polaris franchisees and he brought over six snowmobiles and we rented them to the members to ride around the course. Everything was going along just fine until one day when the S&L owner sent over one of his assistants and his wife for a ride around the course. This was at night, after work and I decided that I should take the wife with me because I knew the course pretty well. We hit the sixth fairway and hit a series of depressions and mounds and after we came through the wife taps me on the shoulder and says that she thinks that she hurt her back coming through the last dip. I asked if she wanted to go back to the clubhouse and she says no, we should go on. A few minutes later she taps me on the shoulder again and says it really hurts and we'd better go back. We get up to the clubhouse and her husband and I get her into the car and he takes her to the hospital. The next morning he calls and tells me that she has a broken back! Up until that time I had been scheduled to race for Polaris in the "Land of the Midnight Sun" race in Alaska. That broken back put an end to my snowmobiling career. We did make money on the venture, though. As a result of our success, that golf course went from seriously in the red to substantially in the black. It takes a few trick shots to shoot a good round!

It was at De Kalb that I got to test the first of the riding greens mowers. I was testing it for Jacobson Manufacturing. There were only two problems with that first mower. As I drove down the fairways early in the morning, all of the dogs at the houses along the edges would start to howl. The other problem was that it broke the hydraulic lines. In those days the lines were steel pipe and Jacobson would send me replacement pipes that would arrive on the bus on a regular basis. After a while curiosity got the better of the bus driver and he finally asked me what in the world we were doing with all of that pipe? I told him I'd tell him if he swore to secrecy. He did and I told him that we were building a giant still and if he kept his mouth shut, I give him one of the first bottles! He never said another word.

It took about a year to find out what was causing the hydraulic lines to break. It turned out to be a high-pitched vibration that only dogs could hear! Life around the club was much more pleasant after we cured that little problem.

De Kalb was notable for three other reasons. The first was that our youngest daughter, Robin, was born there. The second was that is where I started using women as laborers on the golf course. This was unheard of in the industry at the time. I found that women are far superior to men in many positions on the staff. They are much more precise and meticulous. I hired several at De Kalb and everywhere I've been since.

The third event of note was a growth that I had removed from my face. I didn't think much about it until a few years ago when I got to looking at it in the mirror one morning and Sue asked if it was all right. I said it was and that was when she told me that the doctor who removed it had given me only four years to live. I didn't know it at the time and I guess I'm happy that I didn't, but even not knowing, I started thinking about all of the chemicals that workers in the industry are exposed to every day. I've seen many laborers, assistant pros and superintendents afflicted with various growths, respiratory problems and other related aliments. Two outstanding individuals whom I had promoted to superintendent have passed away from cancer. In those days we didn't realize that we were poisoning ourselves. That's when I started to look for a better way to handle the problems that we were treating with all of those chemicals. I began to discover biological agents that worked as well or better than chemicals. As you'll see later on, this would eventually change my life.

Emmett Kelly, world famous clown born in Sedan, Kansas

The author putting on sand greens at Sedan Country Club, age 12

 XXI Torneo Nacional Abierto
NOVIEMBRE 1965

Hitting a duck hook in the 1965 Mexico Open

The author with Col. Ralph Wright, Deputy ROTC Camp CDR, First Infantry Division, Ft. Riley, Kansas

Standing next to my favorite airplane, the Stearman, with my friend Arnon. This one was used as a crop duster in Mexico.

My friend the Medicine Man for the Apache Tribe, Milford Yosis

Dr. Carey Middlecoff and Frank Stranahan putting on the 9th green, Kansas City Open

One of my heroes–Chuck Yeager

Drilling rig that I used in Africa

Kicking some shuffleboard ass on a Harley

Having a toast with my Irish friends, Chuck Fox, Joe Whittle and Des O'Brien at the Curragh Golf Course, one of the oldest in Ireland

My friend Victor Mature. The course he refers to is Rancho Santa Fe.

Here is myself and my friend Bill Adams at the National Golf Course Superintendent
Meeting in 1997

From left to right: Yankee legend Whitey Ford, the Bio Reactor and Myself

Chapter 7

Director of Golf for the city of Kansas City, Missouri. The city gave me temporary living quarters in the city's rose garden. The room was in the basement of the meeting center and had an expandable door that partitioned it from the rest of the hall. One morning, soon after I arrived, I was sound asleep when the expanding door started to slide open. It seems that nobody had told the ladies garden society that there was a gentleman using the back half of the room as sleeping quarters. When I woke up and the door was fully opened, there stood about fifty women, waiting for their lecture on the finer points of Bonsai and gasping at the sight of a grown man in bed.

Shortly after I arrived in Kansas City I was approached by one of the players and asked if I was interested in doubling my salary. I asked him what he had in mind. He said that all I'd have to do is order my chemicals and fertilizers and let him go pick them up and his group would give me what they thought that I needed to run the golf course. I politely declined the offer and thought nothing more about it. Some time later I was in Percy's bar, which was down at the end of Swope One, one of the courses I was overseeing. This ol' boy that I knew from around the courses asked me if I'd like to go up to Hillcrest Country Club and have a drink. That sounded pretty good to me so up we went. They brought me a drink and I took about two sips from it and all of a sudden I felt like I was going to pass out. I went down to the men's locker room and decided to take a shower. I felt much better afterward and I got to thinking that it must have been my imagination. As I was getting dressed, here comes this ol' boy looking for me. We go back to the bar and I take another couple of sips of my drink and the same thing happens. Now I don't claim to be the brightest light bulb of the bunch, but sooner or later I figure things out. I excused myself and headed out through the kitchen and started walking back to my truck. It took me two and a half hours to get there and by that time my head was clear and I realized what almost happened. It turns out that there was a fairly large, organized group that was approaching business owners and managers with the proposition that the business order large quantities of whatever supplies they needed. They then would let the group pick up the supplies and deliver a reasonable amount and then the group would keep the rest to sell. Pretty slick operation. These guys were no amateurs. If a person didn't go along with the proposal, the group would drug the target, put him in bed with a whore and take pictures of him. They then would blackmail him. It proved to be pretty effective, except in my case. I was lucky.

Kansas City proved lucky for me in many other ways, too. One day Frank Vaydik, the Director of Parks, (who was then and still is one of my heroes) came to me and asked if I'd like to build a golf course. Now there are those who would be surprised that we considered each other a friend. Frank and I used to argue something terrible. We enjoyed the give and take and remain good friends who like spirited discussions. I remember one Christmas Eve party at the Kansas City city hall, up on the 16th floor. Frank and I were in this hellacious argument. The party started at one in the afternoon and we were still arguing at 12:30 that night. We had been sipping an adult beverage or ten and we were really going at each other. Finally Frank decides he's had enough and starts to leave. I told him that I thought that my car was out at his house. He said "Well you're going to ride in the back seat and not say one damn word or I'll throw your ass out in the street!" We get all the way out to his house and he asks where my car was. I told him that I realized about half way there that I had actually driven it down to city hall that afternoon. So we went into his house, still arguing and finally Frank says "Get the hell out of here. Take my car!" With that he threw the keys at me. When I talked to him the next day, Christmas day, he said that he told his wife that "Runyon doesn't have any sense at all!" His wife said that he had even less. He asked why she thought that and she said it was because "You let him drive your car home last night!"

Frank always admired me because I controlled the "In" and "Out" baskets at city hall. I had discovered that all of the night janitors at city hall played golf. All it cost me was a dozen golf balls to make sure that my piece of paper was no more than third from the top. This guaranteed that I was only three days away at the most. It seems that most city workers in those days worked at the paper-shuffling rate of one project per day.

When Frank made the offer to build the new course I jumped at the idea and he said he had 350 acres and $1,000. It was all mine to do with as I pleased! I figured that a body could always find a way to do things if he just put his mind to it. I contacted the Army Corps of Engineers and asked if they would like to build this course as a training project. They said that they would be very interested in doing the project. The next step was to notify the City Council and get approval to proceed. They were very skeptical as to what the Army would be willing to do, so I set up a meeting between the two parties. Just before the meeting was to take place, the City Council gets a hold of me and tells me that there is only one other thing that is needed to make the project fly; we needed the approval of the Local 101 of the Operating Engineers Union. I set up a meeting and went in and told them of the great need for more parks and more golf courses and the lack of funds to build them. For that reason I was asking the Army to come in and build it as a training project and I'd like their blessing. The president of the Local 101 swelled up and said that there was no way that they were going to allow "that brown shit" to come in to do anything. I got a little hot and told him that it was guys like him and organizations like his that kept us from getting things like this done. He immediately backed off and told me that he didn't want the Army, but his group would like to build the course for me. He said that the Local 101 had a pilot program to train inner-city workers to handle heavy equipment. They'd like to do the same thing that the Army was willing to do. There was only one problem, they had no budget for the fuel required to run the machines. I went back to the Council and told them of the Union's offer and they almost laughed me out of the chambers. It seems that the unions and the city had been at each other's throat for years and nobody could believe that this union would do anything like what I was proposing. I was also aware at the time that the Nixon administration was looking for projects to train the poor inner cities for well paying jobs. I set up a meeting between the parties and don't you know that a deal was worked out between the Nixon administration, the Local 101 and the city of Kansas City and Kansas City ended up with another golf course for the grand sum of $1,000!

That project was memorable for several reasons. At one time I had 125 people being trained to run all manner of heavy equipment. Most of these people were hard-core inner-city residents who had never been given a decent shot at any kind of real work. One cold, blustery November day I drove to the site and see some guys huddled around a 55-gallon drum with a fire blazing away. It's obvious from their actions that an argument is taking place. It seems that several of them thought that they were cheated out of a couple of hours on their paychecks. As I get out of my truck a glue can that had been in the drum exploded. Everyone headed for the trees, drawing a .38 from their hip pockets. That was when I found out that I was the only guy on the project without a gun! I've got to tell you, that's a very lonely feeling!

That group of guys was special, but there was one who was more special. Everyone called him Big Roy. He was about six foot five inches tall and went about 285. I first met Big Roy about two weeks after I started in Kansas City. I had gone through two course rangers within a week. It seems that there was a ninesome that showed up frequently and intimidated the rangers into leaving them alone. We got more flack from the golfers behind them than you can believe. The first time that I laid eyes on Big Roy I knew that I had found my man! I had to explain to him what a course ranger was and what a foursome was, but once he grasped the concept of foursomes, he decided that it might be a pretty good job. I put him in a cart and sent him on his way. About two hours later Big Roy comes back, laughing and smiling. "You won't believe what I just saw out there. A NINEsome!" I allowed that I may have heard of such a problem. He says that a big, black gentleman with white side burns was the leader of the group and when Big Roy pulls up and tells them that ninesomes weren't allowed on the course, this guy comes up and says "Oh, yeah? Who says so?" Big Roy pulls a .38 out of his hip pocket, waves it in Mr. White Side Burns face and says, "Mr. 38 says so!" That was the last time that a ninesome ever played on that course.

Big Roy was a conscientious and loyal worker, let me tell you. Joe Clough, the editor of *Grounds Maintenance Magazine*, wanted to do an article on night maintenance of golf courses. I told him to meet me at the course about 2:00AM and I'd show him everything that we did. I met him out in the parking lot and I looked out over the course to find out where Big Roy was mowing the greens. I couldn't hear the mower and I couldn't see it sitting anywhere. I told Joe that Big Roy must have had trouble and was probably back in the maintenance shed. On our way there, as we passed the fourth hole, something caught my attention out in the water hazard. I looked closer and spotted and white hardhat, white teeth and the whites of someone's eyes. It was Big Roy, up to his neck in water. I called out to him and asked him what the hell he was doing in the middle of the water hazard. "I'm sitting on the greens mower," he says. I asked how long he'd been there and he says "About an hour and a half." When I asked him why he was there he told me "I was scared to leave her, we might never find her again!" After we hauled Big Roy and the mower out of the lake, I asked him how he had managed to get into the lake in the first place. "I was mowing number four and I stopped to light a cigarette," he says, "and you know how there is a lever to go forward and backwards? Well, I just pulled it the wrong way!"

One day about a year later, on a Friday afternoon, as I was driving home from a meeting of the Central Plains Turf Grass Foundation, I heard on the news that Roy Lee Rivers had been arrested for suspicion of shooting and killing his wife. I'll be damned if Big Roy wasn't the first one to work on Monday morning! I didn't say anything and about 10AM he comes into my office and asks if I had heard what he did. I said that I had heard that he killed his wife. He says that's right. "We were in the kitchen," he says, "and we got into a terrible argument and the next thing I knows is that she has pulled her .38 and is taking dead aim at me! It was then that I realized that my .38 was out in the car. I don't remember how I got to my car and gun, but I did and I dropped her right on the front porch. Do you know that when I gets up on the front porch and rolls her over, I found out that I had hit her four times!" Almost a year to the day later the police shot and killed Big Roy in a shoot out on that very same porch. That was the end of one of the best course rangers that I ever had.

So we got the course completed. The design was collaboration between Mike Malyn and myself and we did it with non-appropriated funds and trainee labor. We actually built the seventh green five times! Every time that we got it nearly done, here would come some trainee with a bulldozer and wipe it out! It was named Hodge Park and to this day it is one of the most heavily played courses in the mid-west.

During the construction of Hodge Park we had some extra equipment and trainees from time to time and the city approached me to do the reconstruction on another city course, Penn Valley Lake, in downtown Kansas City. The lake had been there for a long time and the lake had filled in over the years. We decided to dredge the lake and take it back down to its original depth of about 40 feet. As we were getting started an older gentleman approached me and asked what we were doing. I told him and he asked how far down were we planning to go? I said about 40 feet or so. The gentleman told me that I didn't want to do that, that 30 feet would be fine. I said no, I thought that we should establish the original depth. He took me by the arm, looked deep into my eyes and said, "Son, you REALLY don't want to go down more than 30 feet." I was taught to respect my elders and so we stopped at thirty feet. To this day I wonder what was in that next ten feet that had the old gentleman so agitated. I only know that it was something that I definitely did not want to see.

When we first started Penn Valley Lake, everyone told me that we would never get the project done because the locals would steal us blind and/or sabotage the project. It was a pretty rough neighborhood, but I went and looked up one of the main guys and asked him how important it would be to his people if I cleaned up the lake and stocked it so that they could fish on it. He said that would be a pretty good thing and the guys would appreciate it. I told him that I only had one problem. Folks told me that I could never complete the job because I'd get all of my equipment in there and I'd get stolen blind. He asks me if I had a five-gallon can of gas. I said that I did. He said to set it out by the curb and guaranteed me that when the job was done, that five-gallon can of gas would still be there. So I did and it was still there (as well as everything else) when the job was done. I went and asked him how he had done it and he said that he had let it be known that if there were any problems at the job site there would be a mass castration! That's what I call effective security!

About a month or so after we started, it was time to send in my first 30-day report to Washington. No sooner had they received it than four top brass show up at the clubhouse looking for me. And they are really hot. The leader said "Mr. Runyon we think it is commendable that you are teaching the inner-city workers how to operate heavy equipment, but there is something in your report that disturbs us." I asked what that might be. "You state in your report that when these trainees get into a vehicle, they put it in reverse and then look back, thus causing a lot of accidents." I said that was true. "You further state that when an experienced worker gets into a vehicle he looks back first and then puts it in reverse, thus causing fewer accidents." I said that was also true. "Mr. Runyon, we find this very hard to believe. We see a lot of the equipment with the front end dented in." I said "You dumb sons of bitches, who do you think they are backing into?"

The boys from Washington, D.C. were involved because even though the Operators Union 101 was supplying the equipment and trainers, the government was paying the trainee's salary. When we got all through, that program was declared to be one of the most successful of its kind and has become a model for programs ever since.

While we were doing all of the construction and training I started to bring in young interns who wanted to learn to be golf course superintendents. This was the start of a program that I continued wherever I went. It proved to be very successful. There were two guys who were very special at Kansas City. The first was Cary Tegtmeyer. I originally brought Cary in to the program when he was a student at Penn State University Turf School. He started out as an intern and then became an assistant, and then when he graduated he became Head Superintendent at Minor Park Golf Course. He and his brand new bride were living in a converted barn on the edge of the golf course and she, as all new brides are want to do, wanted to have dinner on the table when he got home. She would call every day at four o'clock to see if he would be home at five. Whenever I answered the phone I'd tell her that she'd be lucky to see him TODAY! She eventually got used to it. They are still married and Cary is one of the best in the business.

The other guy was Larry Hanks. Larry started out working summers as an intern while he was going to college at Missouri State. When he graduated I hired him to run the construction of Hodge Park and when I left he was the one who finished the project. I will always be grateful for the fine job that he did. Larry spent many years as a superintendent and now is running a very large golf operation in Florida.

Larry's first day on the job was a doozy! We had been experiencing a rash of small fires around the construction site for the new course. Trashcans, lumber piles, and dry grass – as I said, all small fires. The day Larry arrived we broke for lunch along with the crew and this one guy set fire to the canvas top of a road grater. In trying to set the top on fire he actually set himself on fire. He received third degree burns, mostly on his back and ended up in the hospital. While he was there he got to thinking that one of us had set fire to him. The day that he was released from the hospital he arrived in the parking lot at the course and walked down the path to the maintenance shop with a sawed off shotgun. He apparently focused his rage on a guy that we all called "Sarge" who had been a Master Sergeant in the Army. Sarge sees this guy coming, carrying the shotgun and he calls the police. He just hangs up as the guy steps inside the shop, sees Sarge and starts blasting! Sarge dives behind a greens mower and the guy blows the engine off of the mower. Sarge dove behind another mower and the guy blows away another engine! This went on for six rounds of ammunition. Sarge is about to run out of equipment to hide behind when Larry Hanks, first day on the job remember, walks in on all of this. Larry talked the guy into taking his gun back up to the parking lot and putting it away. About this time the riot squad comes charging over the hill. That guy was so fortunate not to have been blown away by those guys. I think the only thing that saved him was that he had done as Larry suggested and put his gun in his car. If he had that shotgun in his hands, I don't believe he would be alive today. It wasn't much of a welcome to Kansas City for Larry Hanks, but it is one I guarantee he remembers to this day!

There was a time in Kansas City when I thought I might have been in Dodge City instead. I was leaving for a vacation one year and I had just pulled out of the parking lot and started down the main road when I spotted a guy up on the hill with a rifle and he aimed and shot at a car in front of me. The glass shattered and the car ran off the side of the road and hit a wall. I saw the guy run into the woods and disappear and I ran over to the car and found an older couple pretty shook up but otherwise ok. The bullet had gone through the passenger side window and lodged in the dashboard between them. I went around the corner to a pay phone and called the police and then went back up to the clubhouse. When I got to the clubhouse there were two foursomes running up the first fairway and they were very excited. It seems that they had been pinned down in the sand traps on two side-by-side greens by someone shooting at them! Luckily no one was hurt but he sure tore hell out of the two greens! The police told me later that they thought he was using a military rifle such as an M-16. They never did catch the guy, but everyone was a little nervous putting on those greens for a while!

I have discovered that every now and then and golf pro has to keep his game sharp at another course and play, preferably for money, a few rounds with others of his caliber. Every Thursday there was a big money game going on at Staton Meadows Golf Club in Independence, Missouri. Leonard Dawson who was one of the top professional golfers during the '40s ran the game. He was Sam Snead's traveling partner and a real character. He took great pride in telling one and all that he had been married eight times and his eighth and current wife should be real proud of him because he had made her a millionaire. "Yes sir, Larry, she had eight million when I married her and now she's down to one million!" Leonard was also a hustler. I had finished a round one Thursday and I felt pretty good about things since I broke even. When Leonard was running things, you considered yourself way ahead when you broke even. So I was all set to leave when Leonard tells me that I have to stick around and play this special game that the locals played after the course shut down for the day. The game involved standing on the porch, with your back to the pro shop looking at the hedge that is around the putting green. You then would throw a golf ball over your shoulder and up onto the roof. It would come rolling down and wherever it landed, that was where you played it to the designated hole. That first night I lost $500. My ball never got past the hedge. The next Thursday I stayed around to play again and this time I lose $600. I still couldn't get out of the hedge! The third week I went and after 18 holes I started to leave and Leonard stopped me and asked me where I was going. "I'll tell you one place I am NOT going and that is out to play that silly game. I've already lost $1,100!" Leonard says "Goddamn it, Larry, give me $25!" When I asked why, he just insisted that I give him the money. So I did. I went and took my place on the porch, tossed the ball over my shoulder onto the roof and damned if it doesn't land on the green for the first time! That's when I found out that Leonard had a guy on the roof! I won back $500 that day. I won another $500 the next week. Now I was only down $100. I was feeling pretty good about things, especially since I hadn't been in that damn hedge in two weeks and my scratches were almost healed. The first time I had come home with my arms all scratched up, Sue thought I had been in a car wreck! I told her that I had just been trying to play my ball out of a hedge. So the third week I go back, figuring to get ahead of the game. Leonard pulled me aside and told me that his old friend Sarge was in the game, but he didn't have any money and was looking for someone to cash one of his checks. Leonard told me not to take his check, it would bounce higher than a Titleist off a cart path. Sure enough, here came Sarge with his checkbook out. I told him that I just couldn't cash his check. Sarge went around the corner, mad as hell. Before long Leonard grabs me by the arm and says, "Holy shit! Here comes the Sarge and he's got a .38 in his hand!" Everybody scattered for cover and I ended up under my Kansas City owned pickup truck. Leonard managed to join me under there and bullets are flying everywhere. A .38 slug makes a distinctive sound when it hits a pickup truck. It is a special kind of "Thunk" that one does not ever forget. I ended up with 6 thunks in that city owned truck. When I took it into the municipal body shop and they asked about the holes, I told them that I had won six car mirrors in a contest and I had bored six holes. Looking for the right place for them. I decided that I really couldn't use that many mirrors so I wanted them to patch up the holes. I know they didn't buy the story for a minute, but I think that they figured since I went to all the trouble to come up with the story, they would be good enough to go along with it!

It was at Swope Park Number One in Kansas City that I had a life lesson on how dedicated golfers are to the game. There was a foursome that played each and every morning. The youngest member of the foursome was in his early 80s, the oldest was in his 90s. One day I get a call on my radio asking me how they could get an ambulance up on the fairway. They told me that there had been a heart attack and immediately I knew that it was one of the old guys in that foursome. I got to the site about forty-five minutes later and the guy was still lying there! There was an ambulance strike in Kansas City at the time and there weren't enough operating to fill the need. I went down to the clubhouse and the park ranger was interviewing the remaining members of the foursome. One of them was saying that the victim was halfway through his backswing when he collapsed. "We knew he was dead when he hit the ground." They called for the course marshal, who in turn called for the ambulance and the three remaining members continued with their game. "We played his ball out for him," one of the guys told me, "and he got a five on the hole." The park ranger asked him to repeat what he'd just said. "Yeah, we played out his ball and he got a five." I told them that I bet their friend was looking down on them, madder than hell because he bogeyed the hole. "We thought about that," one of them said, "so we went back and played it again and damned if he doesn't get another five!" As I said, golfers are a dedicated lot. They are also fair minded and loyal to their friends.

When I got to Kansas City I had been fighting all of the chemicals and diseases and insects that can affect turf grass. There I was seeing more diseases than I had ever seen before. Pythium was one of them. It is a water borne disease that is spawned by a sterile environment. We were well into USGA sand greens at this time and they were very sterile. I got to talking to other superintendents in the area and we all had pretty much the same problems. Most of the guys blamed it on the weather. I got to pondering and I concluded that it just couldn't be entirely the weather. Weather had a role, certainly, but it was something that we were doing, or not doing. I thought that we must be doing something different than we used to because we hadn't seen these kinds of infestations and infections until just recently. That's when I remembered our Cow Manure Tea and the healthy greens that it produced. The very next day I started on an organic feeding regimen that would eliminate as many chemicals as possible. The results were impressive. The pythium disappeared and I have been on almost a crusade ever since. I started down a path to learn about microbes and microbial action that I still follow to this day.

It was my great pleasure to have made the acquaintance of one of the very top experts in the field of turf grass management, Dr. Fred Graw. He had started the Musser International Turf Grass Foundation and I ended up as one of the first members. The purpose of the foundation was to supply scholarships to young people who wanted to pursue careers in turf grass management. Burt Musser had been a professor at Penn State University Turf Grass School and Dr. Graw had been one of his students. When Musser died, Fred named a foundation after him and we raised the funds to send others to school. Dr. Graw was also the first president of the United States Golf Association Turf Grass Section.

In addition to his unparalleled expertise in turf grass, Dr. Graw was also a pretty fair country writer, which he displayed to my wife Sue frequently. He used to write her what used to be known as "mash" notes and send them to her from all over the country.

I also re-learned something about history and tradition at Minor Park there in Kansas City. Some years earlier, when I was at Lyons, Kansas, I had noticed these big, deep ruts going across the course. I figured that no one had filled them in because there was no money to do it. I began a project to gradually fill them in. Soon after I started about four cars full of old timers came roaring up to me. They all jumped out, screaming for me to stop. "Do you know what you are doing?" one of them asks. I said, sure, I was filling in the ruts so that balls didn't get stuck down in them. "You can't do that!" they said, "That's the Santa Fe Trail!" I quickly dug out the fill that I had put into the ruts left by the pioneers heading west. At Minor Park I discovered another stretch of the Santa Fe Trail that ran directly across the course. I was relaying the story to Frank Vaydick of me trying to fill up the trail in Lyons and what a coincidence I thought it was that here that trail was again. I had done some research on the trail in the meantime and I told him how important the Santa Fe Trail was to American history. I wasn't long before Frank had a monument placed along side the trail marking the spot where so many thousands of hearty souls struck out for the west.

Chapter 8

I guess that this is as good a time as any to explain "Runyon's Four Year Rule" for golf course superintendents and/or golf pros. It seems that there are two distinct groups at almost all country clubs. There are the golfers and there are the socialites. The golfers only care about greens that putt true, sand bunkers that are firm and rough that doesn't resemble a wheat field. The society side of the club cares much more about amenities. Nice landscaping around the clubhouse, color coordinated tablecloths in the dining room, matching plates, coordinated carpeting are all very important. And paint. I have painted more ladies locker rooms more shades of pink than any man on the face of the earth! More superintendents get in bigger trouble because of a bad choice of pink than anything they could possibly do to the course. As far as the Board of Directors is concerned, it is either controlled by the social side or the golfing side. Most superintendents are hired about four years after the social side has seized power and repainted everything in the place. The maintenance budget, of course, has gone to hell at the expense of fertilizer, chemicals, etc. Once the superintendent starts he has about four years to bring the course back to top shape before the social side rises to power once again. The superintendent hates the social side of country clubs. That is why I have never stayed more than four years at any one course. When I find myself talking to painters about another one of the 14 shades of pink for the ladies' locker room for the third or fourth time and the board won't let me buy anything, I know it's time to move on. The golf pro is caught in the crossfire between golf and social. He has the virtually impossible task of getting along with both sides. That is why there is such a huge turnover of golf pros. The best pros are those who can teach and run an efficient pro shop. A successful pro never takes sides. He becomes a consummate diplomat as well as a pretty good golfer. The most damaging individuals to any country club are the general managers. Most GM's get too one sided towards the social. Very rarely do they bother to get to know the golf course maintenance side of the game or what the superintendent's and/or the golf pro's problems are. He knows just enough about those two to be dangerous! To be a successful General Manager takes a rare blending of skills. He or she must not only understand the golf and maintenance but also be expert in the food and beverage side. These rare birds are holding down the cream of the jobs in golf today.

From Kansas City it was time to make move number 34 since Sue and I were married. The moving van people were getting to know us pretty well by this time. Anyway, we got packed up again and headed for the Lodge of the Four Seasons in Lake of the Ozarks, which was owned by a very wealthy businessman by the name of Harold Koplar.

The lake itself is the largest man made lake in North America with something like 2,400 miles of shoreline. The fishing for bass, catfish, perch and crappie was exceptional and the recreational boating was a lot of fun. The countryside was covered with oak trees and made for a beautiful scenery. In the springtime the Dogwood and Red Bud blossom and it is gorgeous. It always reminded me of Sedan, Kansas back home. There was a certain road that was called the Red Bud Tour. Every year people would drive out there and plant seedlings along the road. After a few years that whole road would burst into bloom in the springtime. It was an impressive sight.

After I accepted the job Harold Koplar asked me if I knew where I would be living. I told him that we had been living in city provided housing in Kansas City but we were thinking that if we liked Lake of the Ozarks we may want to buy a place. Harold said that he had a place that we might consider living in, but there were some ramifications, for instance we may have to show it to perspective buyers now and then since it was for sale. I said that since Sue and I were considering buying a place, we may be interested in his, if we liked it. I asked him how much he was asking. You have to remember that I haven't seen this place yet. Harold told me that he was asking $750,000! He asked if I wanted to see it. After I got my wind back I said sure. So off we went and arrived at this mansion that was built by the Union Electric Company when they were building the Bagnell Dam, which formed Lake of the Ozarks. This place was built entirely out of logs, did not have one nail since it was all hand pegged and had thirteen bathrooms! After we moved in we all crowded into one bathroom. That's when I discovered that families follow toothpaste and toilet paper. Where the two are, that's where the family goes. After taking the tour of the place Harold asked what I thought. I told him that I would take the job and would live in the house with an option to buy! And so we executed move number 34. What a place! Our living room was 3,200 square feet with 35-foot ceilings! We were located on a 100-foot bluff above the lake and we had a view down 14 miles of Lake of the Ozarks. There was a chair on a rail that we called the electric chair. It would take you down to the lake and back up. The first night that we were there, Sue woke me up in the middle of the night and told me that there was something in the bedroom with us. I asked her what it was and she said that she wasn't sure, but it had gone into the closet. Sue asked what I was going to do and I told her that I was going to get under the covers! She said that whatever it was there goes another one! My God, it was a bat! That's when we found out that another of the ramifications that Harold mentioned was the fact that a whole colony of bats had taken squatter's rights on the place! There were hundreds of them! Every night when the sun went down, out would come the bats. We had a cat at the time that got rid of all but 15 of those bats. For four years we lived with those 15 bats and they became almost pets to us. One night Sue's dad had come down to visit us and he decided that he wanted to sleep by the fire. The house had this huge fireplace that could accommodate six-foot logs. So we set him up by the fire and we all went to bed. Sometime in the middle of the night I woke up and heard this Godawful clamoring coming from downstairs. I went down and found Sue's dad standing in the middle of his bed with a rolled up newspaper in his hand. "My God, you're not going to believe this one! There are bats in this house!" One of the good things about those bats is that houseguests never stayed very long.

That place was a great party house. At the time I had a good friend by the name of Monty Davidson who was a popular country and western singer. He came down to see the place with an eye to building his own log house. When he got there he noticed that there was a loft at the end of this huge living room that would make a great stage. He told me that he'd love to bring his band down and use that loft to play from. And that is exactly what he did. At the same time there was a guy by the name of Ron Kempker who owned a sand and gravel pit. Ron was an expert on turkey fries and he offered to bring some if I got Monty to play. So I did and the more people who heard about, the more said that they were coming. A day before the party I realized that I hadn't clued Sue in to what was going to happen. I told her that I was going to have a few guys over and she said, "Oh, God, I suppose you're going to have 7 or 8 guys over here!" Well at the time I already knew that there were going to be at least 150! The final count was in excess of 270! It became an annual event. Monty liked the cabin so much that he ended up quitting show biz and building log houses at Lake of the Ozarks.

I should pause here and explain that "turkey fries" are deep fried turkey testicles. Turkeys are castrated in August so that they will fatten up by Thanksgiving. They are considered a delicacy and connoisseurs eat them like popcorn. At one point during that first party I encountered a lady out on the balcony wearing a fur coat. Now it was way too warm for anything close to a fur coat, but she was determined to show it off. As I came up to her she asked, "Mr. Runyon, what part of the turkey did you say these fries were from?" I allowed as I did not recall saying, but they were, in fact, the turkey's testicles. She dropped the one in her hand like it was a snake! I came back to her about 20 minutes later and she had shed her coat and was losing her fries over the banister!

After I got comfortable at the Lodge of the Four Seasons, I accepted an invitation to speak at the University of Massachusetts Turf Conference. Sue decided, for the first time ever, that she wanted to go with me. So off we went to Baltimore, Maryland and checked into the Baltimore Hilton. We settled in for a good night's sleep before the conference started the next day. About four o'clock in the morning we were awakened by the sound of sirens coming from the street below. We were staying on the 19th floor and we looked down on a cold, January night and saw fire personnel running into our building. Sue asked if we were on fire and I told her that we were and we had to get out fast. We opened the door and stepped out into the hallway and immediately became engulfed in smoke. The door had shut behind us and neither of us had thought to bring a key. I learned several lessons for that night, the first of which is to always leave your hotel key in your pants so that you have it with you if you have to get out fast and then back in.

The smoke was so thick in that hall that we could neither see nor breathe. The only clear air that we could find was down almost to the floor. There was a little micro-climate down there that we could breathe in if we crawled on our hands and knees. We began searching for the fire escape. This is where I learned lesson number two. Fire escapes are marked at the top of the door, not at the bottom and so a person cannot find the escape from a crawling position. While we were searching there was a guy running up and down the hallway screaming "Fire! Fire!" in a total panic. We went along and I tried every doorknob that we passed with no luck. About this time Sue decides that she is going to make a run for it and stands up and starts to go. I reached out and caught her foot and pulled her back down where there was at least some air. She told me later that the one thing that flashed in her mind was that she wasn't going to live to see her grandkids. The irony is that here we are, some 30 years later and she STILL hasn't seen any grandkids! She may never see any grandkids!

Anyway, about the third time that we passed the elevators I figured that we didn't have anything to lose and despite all of the advice to the contrary, I punched the down button. It was as if the elevator was waiting for us. As we tumbled into the car, the panic stricken guy who was yelling "Fire!" came by again and I tackled him and the elevator doors closed with the three of us inside. It took us down to the third floor and the doors opened and there was a wall of flames! We had found the fire. The panicked guys yells "Oh, Shit!" real loud. Suddenly a fireman appears in the doorway and yells for assistance. Three firemen appear and throw us over their shoulders and carry us through the flames, down stairs and outside were we are standing in 22 degree January weather. I had heard a strange "Clump, clump" as we were crawling in the hall and I couldn't figure out what it was. As we were standing in the cold I looked down and Sue didn't have any shoes on…but she did have a pair in her hand! The sound that I heard was her shoes hitting the floor as she crawled. A guy standing right next to her was bare foot, also and his feet were turning blue. I asked why he didn't grab some shoes on the way out and he told me "Hell, I'm from California and the last thing I thought about was shoes!" About that time another guy comes walking by and he hasn't got any shoes, either. I said, "Hey, I'll bet you're from California!" He says yes, how did I know? "No shoes!"

They took us all down about a block to another hotel and we were gathered in the lobby, getting warm. As soon as we got there the guy that I had pulled into the elevator found us and he thinks that I have saved his life. He is patting me on the back and telling people how I saved his life. I couldn't get rid of him! About an hour and a half after we got there a woman comes walking by. This guy turns to Sue and says, "My God, there's my wife!" He had forgotten her in the hotel room! She comes walking by and completely ignores him. He follows behind saying "Oh, Honey, I'm glad you're OK!" but she is having none of it. About an hour later they let us go back to our original hotel to get our things. As we entered the lobby we noticed the man and his wife sitting on opposite ends of a big long bench, facing away from each other. I think that it is entirely possible that the very worst thing that I could have done for that guy was save his life! He'd have been better off with a quick death. This way was going to be long and slow and torturous!

The third lesson that I learned was to stand at my room door and see where the closest Fire Exit is. The next thing I do is pace off the distance from my room to the escape. I do it with my eyes open going to the escape and with my eyes closed coming back.

The biggest casualty of that night was Sue's one and only, forever, Mink coat. Sam Brody of Brody Coat Manufacturing of De Kalb, Illinois had given it to her. We tried everything we could think of to get the smoke smell out of those clothes, to no avail.

We took a bus down to Washington D.C. to see Bill and Ree Wilson, our friends from Parsons, Kansas, who were both working for the Department of Transportation at the time. The first thing that Bill says is "Where the hell have you two been? You stink to high heaven! It must be Larry because Sue would never smell that bad!" Since we had arrived just at lunchtime, we went into the cafeteria and as we were standing in line the fire alarm goes off! The authorities evacuated the building and as we were standing out side Bill turns to me and says, "We aren't going back in with you!" And they didn't either!

That was the first and last time that Sue ever went on a business trip with me!

I had two courses at Lake of the Ozarks. The first was a nine-hole layout that had been there forever. The second was an 18-hole course that was designed by Robert Trent Jones. Harold Koplar, the owner who put us in the mansion, approached me to come up with some way to attract attention and get some people to come down our way and stay at the lodge. Well, that first winter was a "once in a hundred years" winter. The Lake of the Ozarks froze over for the first time in 41 years! When I saw that I got to thinking that I could go down right below our house and tee up a golf ball and go for a world's distance record! I called up all of the newspapers in the area and all of the TV stations and all of the radio stations and tell them that I am going to attempt a world record of hitting a golf ball. I enlisted the help of the chief of security for the lodge and he placed a man at each five-mile marker on the lake for the first 20 miles. Each of these men had a radio. I instructed the chief of security that when the first lookout sees the ball go by he is to radio in that the ball is past the five-mile marker. Then when the second guy sees it go by, he is to radio in and so on. The chief says, "What if they don't see it go by?" I said, "Goddamn it! Let me tell you one more time. WHEN he sees it go by, he radios in." He persisted, "But what if the second guy doesn't see it?" I spoke very slowly and clearly, "They WILL see it go by, understand? And they WILL call in." The day of the event there was media from all over that showed up. I was amazed because the roads were bad and it had been storming. I couldn't get any of my family to go down and watch because they are all convinced that this is going to be a tragedy and a family embarrassment! So I get down there and there is a fierce wind blowing down the lake, right into my face! There is no way to hit the ball down the center of the lake, so I decide to hit it across the lake towards the Lake of the Ozark, Missouri boat marina. I told the chief to go over there with his radio and call in when he sees the ball go past him. I allowed as this probably wasn't going to be a world's record, but it will be a state record. The chief wanted to be sure he had all of the bases covered and he asked, yet again, what he should do if he didn't see the ball. I handed him 3 Titleists and sent him on his way with the admonition that when he sees me swing he is to wait and one way or the other he will have a ball over there. The light behind his eyes started to come on about then and he headed off towards the marina. I teed up a new Titleist and hit the first ball right on the screws. It took off across the ice, headed directly for the marina, about a mile and a half away. I had the radio turned way up so the media could hear and pretty soon the radio crackles and the excited voice of the chief comes on. "Here it is! It's bouncing all over these Goddamn boats and I didn't even have to throw a Goddamn ball down!" That story got picked up by the Associated Press and made almost every paper in the country.

During that same winter I had a floating pump dock that became frozen into the lake. The lake was used to generate electricity through the damn, so even though the top was frozen, the water was continuously being sucked out from underneath. The pump dock is frozen in the ice on top of the water and we were trying to figure out how thick the ice was and how high the boat dock was above the water level. We had a helicopter pilot who gave folks tours during the season who told me that he would find out how thick the ice was. He flew his chopper out over the lake and took his skid and hit the ice in several places. As I am watching him his skid breaks through the ice and throws him all off kilter. He overcorrects as he pulls up and the tail goes down and his tail rotor hits the ice and shears off. He goes up into a spiral and then nosedives straight down and through the ice. I was maybe a quarter-mile away and there was nothing that I could do to fish him out. Pretty soon he pops to the surface and climbs out of the water. I got to talk to him about the crash as he is warming up and he says that he is going to use engine failure as his reason for crashing. About that time a film crew from Channel 12 in St. Louis (which was owned by Harold Koplar) comes in and tells him that they filmed the whole thing from the other side of the lake! There went the engine failure reasoning! That pilot survived but his flying career didn't!

I used to play shuffleboard for recreation, amusement and profit. That is to say I would pick up some spending cash in my favorite bar in Lake of the Ozarks. I got so good at it that the regulars wouldn't play me unless I had a handicap. This one day a group of Harley riders came into the place and I came up with the idea of playing all comers while sitting on a Harley! The owner of the place was one of the guys betting against me, so he says fine, let's do it. I went over to the Harley group and asked if one of them would like to split a bet with me if I could use their bike. One guy liked the idea and went outside, fired up his Harley and rode on in. I'd get on the back and shoot my round, and then he'd fire it up, smoke everybody out, go outside, turn it around and come back in. All I did was beat their ass like a drum!

Not long after we arrived in Lake of the Ozarks I decided that I wanted to rebuild a boat that was for sale. It was a beauty that had fallen on tough times. Made out of Mahogany, it was a 28 foot cruiser with twin screws and 90 horse power Hercules engines. I took in a couple of partners on this venture, one of which was my old buddy Percy, who had owned Percy's Bar next to Swope's golf course in Kansas City. After we got it rebuilt, Percy and some friends came down to take the boat out for a spin. While they were out they had a head-on collision with another boat. When the water patrol showed up at our door, Sue was just getting out of the shower and goes to the door with her hair still wet and a towel in her hand. The patrol wanted to know if I had been out in my boat. All the time they are looking at Sue with her wet hair and a towel and she tells them that we hadn't been out in the boat. They didn't believe a word of it! It turns out that Percy had been in the accident and we needed to do a little more rebuilding! That is when I started to learn the wisdom of the old adage that the two happiest days of a boat owner's life are the day he buys it and the day he sells it. In between you spend most of your time cleaning the boat after your friends have been visiting. Boats are in the same category as airplanes and swimming pools. They sound like a great idea before you buy them and pretty soon it sounds like an even better idea that you sell them!

I learned a lot at Lake of the Ozarks. During my five-year stay I worked with and around Buffy Mariah, a famous Japanese landscaper who had worked in Hollywood for Cecil B. DeMille. I worked right beside him and studied everything that he did. One day I found him standing by some new landscaping, cussing in Japanese and jumping up and down. I asked what was wrong and he said, "Got lock upside down!" I was a bit bewildered until I saw that he was pointing at a rock. I asked him how the hell a rock could be upside down? Buffy says, "You dumb American, you don't know that locks have tops and bottoms?" I allowed, as I didn't know that. After working with Buffy for a while I learned to tell the difference between a right side up rock and an upside down rock. To this day when I see a landscape with rocks upside down it upsets me!

Buffy had an assistant by the name of Jed Duncan, a big ol' fella who Buffy would get into arguments with on a regular basis. One day Jed found a big piece of Styrofoam floating in the lake. It had been there a while and was dirty and weathered. It looked just like a rock. Jed brought it back to the course and placed it among the landscaping. He waited for the next argument with Buffy, which wasn't long. He went over to the rock and picked it up, telling Buffy "I've had it! I'm not taking anymore BS from you!" With that he throws the Styrofoam rock at Buffy. Buffy about had a heart attack! He went over to a bench, sat down, lit a cigarette and after four or five puffs went home. He had had it for that day.

That course was an extremely difficult one to maintain. It was built on rock with the topsoil hauled in and placed on top. A superintendent by the name of Gary Grigg was the construction superintendent on the project and he used something like $150,000 worth of dynamite to build the course! They built the sand traps with dynamite and jack hammers. In addition it had a terrible irrigation system. Made by Johns Manville, the system had decoders in each outlet and water would collect around them and short them out and they would quit working. We filed suit against Johns Manville and the trial was held in St. Louis. We were all sitting in a pew on one side of the courtroom and the Johns Manville people were all in a pew on the other side. The judge says to me, "Son, now I want you to tell us in your own words what is wrong with this system." I told him that there was only one thing wrong, "Judge, that system is allergic to water!" He thought that was pretty funny and he roared with laughter. I looked across the aisle and the Johns Manville folks apparently didn't have much of a sense of humor because they were all stony faced. The laugh was on us, though, since we lost the suit!

At this same time Johns Manville had taken out ads on the back of all of the trade publications, advertising their binary irrigation system. The ads featured the superintendent of one of the premier courses in Los

Angeles. I decided to fly out and find out how he could make his system work and I couldn't get mine to do anything. I walked into his maintenance shop, unannounced, and introduced myself. I told him that I was there to discover his secret to operate the system. He looks around and says, "Raise your right hand!" I did and he swears me to secrecy as to what he is about to show me. He takes out a set of keys and opens a big door. Behind the door was a big blue panel, just like I had back in Lake of the Ozarks, with flashing lights and buttons and dials. It was a thing of beauty! He takes out another key and opens the blue panel. There behind the Johns Manville system was a complete Toro irrigation system! He says, "I can't get the damn thing to work, either!"

At the very same time I discovered that I was the very first superintendent in the nation to be infested with an Ataenius beetle. This was not an honor that I was proud of since this little pest ate everything in sight. It has since eaten its way across the country and arrived in California a few years ago. The top expert in infestations at the time was my friend from the United States Golf Association Greens Section, Dr. Fred Graw. I called him up and asked him to help me with my beetle problem. The first thing that we did was to clear a one-foot square patch and then we needed to find out how many larvae were in that square foot. At the time we had a bartender named Mandy who was a Playboy Bunny, amply endowed and a real nice gal. I went into the bar and asked her to bring out all of the swizzle sticks that she could carry. We all got down on our hands and knees and stuck a swizzle stick next to each larva that we found. Pretty soon we had a swizzle stick forest! The only way that we got rid of the little critters was to spray insecticide over the entire course from helicopters. When we finally got the beetles under control, we replanted the entire course in Bermuda grass.

One of the perks of being a golf professional is that you get to meet a lot of famous people. Charles Kuralt stopped by one time when he was doing his road trip across America. Neil Armstrong also dropped by. One of the most memorable people, however was baseball announcer Buddy

Blatner, perhaps best known for being Dizzy Dean's partner on the Game of the Week. Buddy had retired by the time I knew him and owned a house not too far from the golf course. He had endless stories to tell about Dizzy Dean, most of them true! One of his favorites was about an afternoon game they were broadcasting out of St. Louis. The camera was panning around the stands between innings and it kept coming back to a couple that were getting more and more amorous as the game progressed. About the sixth inning Dizzy tells Blatner that he about has the couple figured out. "Buddy," he says, "I've been a watching that young couple during the game and it is obvious that they have a system going for them. He kisses her on the strikes and she kisses him on the balls!" Blatner almost had a heart attack! Off the air, Buddy asked Dizzy what he was thinking of when he made that remark. "Hell, Buddy, the big shots in New York told me to just talk about what I see and that's what I saw!"

Chapter 9

Move 35 in our married life happened when we bought a farm near Lake of the Ozarks. We lived there for a couple of years until I decided that the four-year cycle was about to catch up with us. I was 39 years old, my oldest daughter had just been married on the farm and we had that settled in feeling. Time to move!

I had been negotiating with the Mescalero Apache tribe to run their golf course in Mescalero, New Mexico. Things got to the point where the tribe wanted me to come out and see the course and meet the people involved. They wanted to know if there was an airstrip close by that they could land their corporate jet on. I told them that the field at Eldon, Missouri was being rebuilt and I didn't know if it was ready yet. They checked it out and called back and said that even though it wasn't officially open, it would be all right to land there and pick me up. I knew that this re-opening was a big deal to the town fathers because I had been down to the town barber and they were all talking about it. All of the big wigs in town who owned airplanes were arguing as to who the first one to land on the new strip would be. I was an avid listener since I loved airplanes and was interested in what would happen. On the day that the Apache jet was to arrive to take me to the course, the town scheduled the big ribbon cutting ceremony to officially dedicate the airport. The mayor was there, the high school band was there, the FAA was there, and it was a big deal. They had the plane that was finally chosen as the first one to take off and land set just behind the ribbon. As the speeches concluded and the ribbon was about to be cut I looked up and here comes the Mescalero Apache corporate jet with the Apache symbol on the tail along with the name of the tribe. Wendell Chino, the chief of the tribe, was on board and his own pilot was at the controls. The pilot executes a perfect three-point landing and taxis right up to the ribbon. My son, Larry, had driven me to the airport and I said goodbye to him, took my suitcase, crawled under the ribbon, turned and waved to the crowd and got on the airplane! The chief asked me what was going on as we were rolling down the runway to take off. I told him that they were celebrating the very first landing and take off at the new runway and we were it! I suggested that we fly back over the field at a low level and rock our wings. The chief thought that this was a pretty good idea, and told the pilot what we wanted to do, so he performed what I thought was a beautiful salute maneuver in front of the assembled dignitaries. About a week later when I returned home I stopped by the barbershop and found out that the assembled dignitaries didn't take kindly to a golf course superintendent and an Indian tribe beating them to the punch. Were they pissed off! It was a good thing that it worked out with the Apaches because I don't think that I would have lasted much longer at Lake of the Ozarks!

Inn of the Mountain Gods, in Mescalero, New Mexico, was and is one of the most beautiful golf courses in the world. It is run by Chief Chino who is a shrewd businessman and a former Baptist minister. Now there is a combination for you! He was the father of Indian gambling casinos on the reservations. He likes to brag that the Apache is the only tribe that has yet to sign a treaty with the white man. There are many reasons that I respect the Apache and their courage and dignity with respect to the treaty is a large one.

The Apache had gotten my name from Washington, D.C. because of my work in Kansas City with the training program. They were looking for someone who could handle the maintenance of an 18-hole golf course and also handle the problems associated with minorities.

My job was to get Apaches to comprise at least 22% of the golf course workforce. Chief Chino needed to do this so that he qualified for more money from Washington so that he could expand the facilities.

I should stop and explain a bit about the Apache and the problems on the reservation. It is true that there is a tremendous problem with liquor abuse. Times were tough and there wasn't a lot to do on the reservations. The leading cause of death on the reservation at that time was being run over on the highway. People would wander out on the highway in front of oncoming traffic and be hit, especially at night. Things have changed, as I understand it, now that casinos have provided more jobs. Less unproductive time has allowed the Apache to reassert their dignity, industriousness and honor.

My immediate boss was a gentleman by the name of Milford Yosis, who was also the tribe's Medicine Man. He was a big man who was one of the soberest people that I've ever met. His son was my chief mechanic and, unfortunately, was not one of the soberest individuals that I've ever met! Milford and I devised a plan to get the workers up in the morning after a hard night of drinking. Each morning we would fill a 5 gallon bucket with ice water and go house to house and splash the cold water on the sleeping workers. We always started with Milford's son. They finally got tired of it and started showing up for work on time. While I was there, there were about 2,300 surviving Apaches, including the grandson of Geronimo. The average life span was 33 years. One day Milford came to me and told me that George, one of our workers, wouldn't be in that day. As a matter of fact, he said he wouldn't be in the next day, either. George, he said, wouldn't be in at all. He had been run over the night before. "Now there are only 2,299 Apache!" The Apache still doesn't trust many white men, for obvious reasons, but once they got to know me, we got along just fine. About this time I started wearing a brace on my leg for the first time in several years. The Apache named me "Iron Leg" as a sign of respect. They also had another name for me that was not quite so flattering. All my life I have had bladder problems and as a result I make frequent trips to the bathroom. I quickly attracted the name "Chief Little Bladder." I liked "Iron Leg" better.

Never let anyone tell you that Indian medicine doesn't work. Once when I had a cold Milford asked if I'd like to try a medicine man's remedy. I said I'd try anything. He brought me a concoction that knocked my cold out in a matter of hours! It was amazing! I told him that he had to patent that stuff. He told me that it was a mixture of different plants but that he hadn't found anyone to pass his secrets on to. I heard that he passed over a few years ago without ever passing on his knowledge.

We had some unique problems at Inn of the Mountain Gods. One of the biggest was keeping 1,000-pound elk off of the greens! You can't believe the divots that elk hooves leave in a golf green! We were constantly having to roll and repair greens after an elk herd moved through. We also had a bear problem. The black bear is sacred to the Apache and isn't hassled at all. They come and feed out of the trashcans and cause an unholy mess. On the other hand owls are representative of evil and are practically shot on sight. So hated is the owl by the Apache that there is a bar on the outskirts of the reservation named The Owl Bar that has over 500 stuffed and carved owls in it because the owner doesn't want Apache business. It works.

Being a good golf pro sometimes involves more than just golf and greenskeeping. It takes being part counselor, part diplomat and, on occasion, part minister. At Inn of the Mountain Gods I was faced with my first request for burial on the course. It must be remembered that the course is owned by the Apache and they have never signed a treaty with the white man. They didn't think much of the white man 100 years ago and they still don't think much of him today. But they love to take his money.

One day I was approached by Mona, the wife of one of our more prominent guests. She told me that Alex, her husband, had passed away suddenly and in his will he had requested to be cremated and his ashes scattered on the Inn of the Mountain Gods Golf Course. I explained to Mona how the Apache felt about the whites and that I didn't think she could get permission. She told me that her idea was to hire a plane and dump the ashes from the cockpit. I told her that I thought that if she just went ahead and did it, no one would be the wiser. So she did. A week later she returned and told me that she had attempted the burial. "Attempted?" I asked. She said that she hired a plane and she, her minister, Alex, and the pilot took off. They got up over the course and were admiring the view and she was thinking how happy Alex was going to be in such a beautiful resting place. When the time came she opened the window and tossed out Alex. That was when Alex decided to come back in! He was everywhere! On their clothes, in their hair, in their noses, in their ears and Mona said that she even had some of Alex in her mouth! "I didn't ask the others about Alex being in their mouths, they were upset enough."

As soon as they landed at Alamogordo Airport the pilot called for a maintenance worker to bring a vacuum cleaner. As she was walking away when it was all done, she remembered thinking that Alex was really going to be pissed off. Here he wanted to be buried at Inn of the Mountain Gods, one of the most beautiful places on earth, and he ends up in a vacuum cleaner bag in Alamogordo Airport!

For the first six months at Inn of the Mountain Gods I lived alongside the course. Everyone thought that I was wealthy. Actually it was part of my deal with the Apache. Sue and the kids stayed back at the farm in Missouri until we found a house that we liked. We finally found one down in Tularosa. Sue just hated the house at first. It was a well-built house but it was really run down. We spent the first month fixing it up. It had a pool that was the largest privately owned pool in the state of New Mexico. It measured 62 feet by 65 feet and it took two weeks to fill it. The city water department told me that when I got ready to refill the pool the next year, I should let them know in advance!

This is where I got involved in drilling rigs. I decided to drill a well at our new house and I ran across a guy by the name of Skip Pipper. He was building these little drilling rigs at a filling station in town. I bought one and got to know Skip pretty well and ended up working with him on design and manufacturing. He, in turn, would recommend me to people who wanted wells drilled. I ended up moonlighting and hiring guys to run the rig for me.

There was another golf course close by named Cree Meadows that was owned by a couple of friends of mine, Bob Hickson and Wally Dahlenbach. They asked me to come up and drill a test hole to see if they had water on the property. We hit some real good water, which made a huge difference not only to the condition of the course, but also to the value of it. Later on, when they sold the course, the well was worth $1,000,000 to them.

I had an intern from Purdue University by the name of Jim Davis. He was an outstanding student and when he was about to graduate he had several offers, mine being the worst. He decided that Inn of the Mountain Gods was where he wanted to begin his career and so he told me that he would be out as soon as he graduated. He assumed that he would be staying in the four star hotel on the property. Man, was he wrong. By this time we were really busy, the hotel was full and play on the course was heavy. I was living in a house with several of the golf pros and when Jim showed up I took him up to get squared away. As we were getting out of the car this ol' gal comes up and tries to collect the rent off of him! I explained to her that he wasn't the one to talk to since this was his first day. We walked into the house and the first thing Jim says is "What the hell is that smell?" I told him it was dirty clothes. It seems that the pros would pull a shirt out of the cellophane, wear it for two or three days, toss it in the corner and get another shirt. They never did any laundry. I told him that he would get used to it, I had. We had him assigned to the basement and when he went down to see it, it was pitch black. There were no lights down there! Every night when he went to bed, he laid out his clothes in sequence so that he could put them on in the dark the next morning. The other amenity missing from that house was a functioning shower. We would use the locker room shower at the club each morning. Jim was there for a couple of weeks when he went back to Lafayette, Indiana to get married. When he returned with his bride I asked him if he would like to show her where he had been living. He reluctantly agreed and I drove to the spot. Jim looked around and with a very bewildered expression on his face asked where the house was. "It blew up!" I told him. It was such a huge explosion that the place didn't even catch fire! It blew the limbs off of the big pine trees on the property and pieces were found at the airport, over a half-mile away! My first thought when I had heard about it was that those damn shirts finally went up! It turned out that what Jim had smelled was actually a gas leak. Luckily no one was in the house at the time, not even the landlady trying to collect the rent. The pros were kind of relieved since they didn't have to do the laundry!

The mountain behind the course was called "Sierra Blanca" and was considered sacred by the Apache. When it was proposed that a ski resort be built on the mountain, the tribal council decided that only half of it was sacred. The other half would make a great ski run! Between the beautiful ski area that they built and the most beautiful golf course anywhere, this was paradise. When I arrived at Inn of the Mountain Gods I had perfected my program of organics to the point that I was using about 70% organic and 30% chemicals. This was good, but I wanted to improve as much as I could. The golf pro, Jack Worlick, really liked my efforts to eliminate chemicals as much as possible. Most folks don't realize it, but one of the biggest hazards to people who work at and around most courses is their shoes. Heavy doses of chemicals are picked up in the soles and transmitted to the feet of the workers. Obviously this can be very dangerous. Workers should be warned to wear rubber soled shoes or rubber boots. As I have said, I've lost several friends to cancer and related diseases and I just know that exposure to some pretty toxic chemicals has played a large role in their deaths.

Chapter 10

Towards the end of my four-year rule at Inn of the Mountain Gods I got a phone call from Bill Eschenbrenner, the golf pro from El Paso Country Club. He was inquiring as to whether I might be interested in coming down and taking over as superintendent. I told him that I would be interested but before we went any further the Code of Ethics of the Golf Course Superintendent's Association of America required that I determine the status of the current superintendent. He informed me that "Any superintendent who pisses in my washing machine is not going to be superintendent of El Paso Country Club!" I allowed as that I might require more information. He related that he had a party for Lee Trevino and his wife at Bill's house and had invited way too many people. Every room was jammed, including the laundry room. He had invited the current superintendent out of courtesy even though Bill knew that he was into the sauce pretty heavily by 9:30 every morning. About 10 o'clock that night, Lee Trevino, his wife and the mayor of El Paso are standing in the laundry room when the superintendent comes in, lifts the lid to the washing machine and pisses in it! He obviously thought that he was in the bathroom. I started a month later.

Bill Eschenbrenner is one of those people in the golf industry for whom I have a great deal of respect for their business ability. Among other things, he was one of the first certified golf professionals in the country. He also will forever be known as the guy who got Lee Trevino his tour card. The guys on the tour at the time didn't think much of Lee's background at driving ranges and municipal courses and wouldn't let him come out on the tour. Bill fought to get Lee's experience accepted and then to get a card issued to him.

Shortly after arriving at El Paso Country Club we had a new scoreboard built. Over by the old one there was a mortar that Bill, when we had a shotgun start, would drop an aerial bomb into. One day we were having a lady's tournament and Bill goes out to drop his aerial into his mortar and it isn't there! He sent a maintenance worker over the shop to see if it was there. The worker found it and brought back. Eschenbrenner told him to stick it in the ground and dropped the bomb down the pipe. When he does, the mortar sways because it isn't too stable and fires off and lands in a tree behind the 10th tee. There are two foursomes of women standing there and suddenly they are being showered with branches and leaves and sparks from the bomb. There was a drainage ditch beside the tee and those women started bailing out into it. I got there just as they were picking themselves up and trying to clean the mud and debris from their hair and clothes. Luckily no one was hurt, but they figured that they were going to finish last in the tournament and it was all my fault!

Bill really had a problem with ladies' tournaments and that mortar. The way it worked was that he would light the fuse on the bomb and then drop it into the mortar and off it would go. There was this one time when it was a real windy day and Bill had a terrible time trying to get the bomb lit. Finally he was down to his last match and he was huddled around the mortar, attempting to block the wind and light the bomb. What he didn't know was that he actually had the fuse lit and it went off! Again, luckily he wasn't hurt too bad, but he was shook up pretty good. He went into the locker room and washed up to get ready to award the prizes to the tournament winners. That was when he noticed that he only had one eyebrow left! The bomb had singed off his left eyebrow. Suzy who worked in the pro shop painted him a new one for the awards.

By the time I reached El Paso I was really into finding ways to clean up water. I especially was studying and using a lot of microbes to create higher microbial activity. I had discovered that various microbes eat various things and there might be an organic solution for a lot of the turf problems. I ran into a guy by the name of Al Golf who was growing microbes using the clyristrum from a cow that had just had a calf. His dad had developed the product when he was gold mining down in Mexico. He discovered that it would eat the sulfides that held the gold to the ore. They noticed that the water runoff from the treatment was making the foliage greener than any of the rest of the plants. It was one of the first microbial products that I used on turf grass. I started using that and started seeing even better results. I actually was using a fraction of the chemicals that I had in the past. The more I used this mixture, the fewer problems that I had from diseases. One of the concoctions that we made at the time was what I called Oxywater. A funny thing about that mixture was that if you put it on your face you'd get a tingling sensation and then a cooling sensation and then when you touched your face it felt as smooth as a baby's butt! Later on at Odessa, Texas there was this young locker room attendant who had real bad acne. I gave him a gallon of the oxywater and told him to wash his face with it every day and his acne would go away. Several years later I was playing golf with Texas football coach Darryl Royal and we were sitting in the 19th hole and this guy comes up to me and introduces himself as one of the assistant pros there at Barton Ranch. He says, "You don't recognize me do you?" I allowed as I did not. He told me he was the kid in the locker room with the acne. He asked me what I thought and I said, "Hell! You're beautiful!"

From El Paso I went up to Santa Theresa, which was Lee Trevino's course where it was rumored that he had lost $5,000,000. The course was owned by Charlie Crowder. It was said that Lee owed the IRS somewhere around $700,000 and had no money to pay it. Lee decided to walk away from the course and his partnership with Crowder and Charlie took over the course.

One of the reasons that I went to work for Charlie was that Sue and the kids were still living in Tularosa and Charlie promised to find us a nice place to live. When I arrived at Santa Theresa the course was in shambles. The gophers had chewed up the hydraulic lines of the irrigation system to the point that the whole system was 80% inoperative. The electric bill on the pumping stations was running about $48,000 a month. The first thing I did was rebuild and refurbish the pumps which had rusted to the point of non-performance. Once the pumps were in working order the electric bill went from $48,000 to $8,000 a month!

Charlie had heard that I was pretty good at building waterfalls and he asked me to build a tennis complex with 12 courts and a waterfall or two. This was an interesting project. I never drew up any blueprints or plans of any kind. I would go out each morning with a paint gun and mark out on the ground what we were going to do that day. We ended up building the 12 courts with a quarter mile long waterfall that dropped 80 feet down through the complex. I imported 400 palm trees from Arizona to plant around the waterfall. I had studied the micro-climate in the area and decided that the trees should do well. Charlie questioned the wisdom of palm trees in that area and I assured him that they would live. "They better," he told me, "because if they die, you die!" I said, "Let me take another look!" I did and we went ahead and planted the 400 palms and they are flourishing to this day.

Charlie came to me one day and said that he had a house that Sue and I might like. He said that the only problem was that the house was all-solar and there was a smell that he hadn't been able to get rid of. I went down and saw the house and decided that Sue would like it and told Charlie that I would love to live there. He said that Manuel, one of the maintenance crew, would come down before winter to look at the heating system, since that was where the smell was apparently coming from. Sue and the kids and I moved in and late fall I asked Manuel if he was coming down to check out the heating system. He said "No." I asked why and he told me that he used to be in charge of the kitchen help at the club and one day a young man who was a dishwasher called him and seemed very agitated. The kid wanted to come and talk to Manuel. Manuel told him to come on up. "That was three years ago," Manuel told me, "I am still waiting to see him. He never showed up! And he has a couple of checks that he never picked up. I think that's him buried in the floor of your house!" I told Charlie and he suggested that we dig up the floor and find out. The next morning Manuel showed up with a crew and we got the carpet rolled back and discovered a huge galvanized steel vault that contained the rocks for the solar heating system. It was obvious that someone had cut the top off of it and tried to weld it back, but had done a really poor job. The crew broke for lunch about that time and never came back. They didn't want any part of the search. Sue came and got me and took me out to the backyard and showed me a depression that she noticed. It looked exactly like a grave that had settled. I told Sue that I was going to dig it up and find out what was going on. If nothing else, I told her, we could put a garden in the spot. As I turned over the first few spades of dirt I got a spooky feeling and changed my mind and put the dirt back in place. When we got back in the house I told Sue that we had to get the hell out of there! And we did. I never did find out if there was a body there or it was an elaborate scheme to get us out so that someone else could move in.(Click here to input the text of your first chapter or other division.)

Chapter 11

After Santa Theresa I worked in another part of the golf industry for a year or so.- We moved to Olathe, Kansas to redesign and rebuild drilling equipment with my old friend Buck Rogers who owned Olathe Manufacturing. Buck and his brother Roy (really) were the innovators of most of the golf course maintenance equipment such as seeders, leaf pickers and the like. Buck was an absolute genius as far as machinery was concerned. I could give him an idea for a piece of machinery and he would have a prototype built in 48 hours! Buck is still famous in the industry. Buck and Roy eventually sold out to Jacobson Manufacturing.

I had been working with Buck for years, giving him my ideas about how new equipment should be designed and built for the golf course maintenance industry. I took the rig that I was using back with me and we completely redesigned it and put it back on the market. After a while I got homesick for a golf course and we moved yet again, this time to Arizona City, Arizona. We lived on the 18th fairway and had a great time. I wasn't involved with the course at all since I was spending all of my time on the drilling rig designs.

I had been studying the water problems associated with golf courses for a number of years and water problems in general for a year or two. I came to the conclusion that we were absolutely destroying our fresh water supplies in this country. I also did a study on the six year drought in Africa and I hit upon a solution for the shortage of water there.

I concluded that we should use satellite photography to find the fissures in the granite, which was underneath a five-foot overburden in South Africa. Because the bedrock was granite and it was so close to the surface, there had never been an attempt to do any deep drilling for water. It was assumed that there was little, if any, water to be tapped.

My theory was that there was water in the fissures of the granite. I thought that the fissures could be located by the satellite photos and then photographed using infrared film. Water in any significant quantity would show up as a red plume on the photograph. I figured that if any of these water-carrying fissures coincided with any of the small villages out in the brush, we could drill into the granite and provide water for them. The Department of Commerce invited me to go over to South Africa and teach the locals how to use the drilling rigs. I was working with Olathe Manufacturing as a consultant by this time and they shipped a drilling unit over to use as a training aid. The up shot was that excellent water was discovered in many locations that no one had suspected was there.

I almost didn't make it to Africa because of an incident that happened in Las Vegas, Nevada. My old buddy Buck Rogers and I went out to Vegas to attend the 1984 National Turf Conference. During one of the rare down times, I found myself in the casino with my $50 bankroll. Also I have had enough to drink so that I am totally bullet proof! Money, at that point, meant nothing- probably because I didn't have much. Anyway I found myself standing at a crap table at the Desert Inn and watching this guy roll the dice. Every now and then he would roll and I would hear the crowd go "Oh, Wow!" and everybody looks at me! I didn't know why they were staring, but I was polite and smiled back at them. Finally, after this guy throws four or five times and the crowd has gotten bigger and bigger, the stick man, who I had gotten to know, says "Mr. Runyon, are you really going to let all of that ride again?" I said something semi-intelligent like "What?" He told me that all of the chips in the middle of the table were mine. I looked and they were all black chips. Even in my bulletproof state I knew that black chips were pretty big money. I told the stickman that I thought that maybe we should drag those chips in. He counted it up and there was $48,020! I had put $20 on "Any Crap" which paid seven to one odds and there were a lot of boxcars and snake eyes being tossed. It didn't take very long for the money to add up, in fact it was only four rolls. So I cashed in my chips and went to a local bank and made a deposit. It was then that I discovered that the secret to winning was to have enough money so that you didn't care if you won or lost. It is when you need the money that Lady Luck goes Dixie on you. I couldn't do anything wrong for the rest of the week. The first thing that I did was call Sue and tell her that I was going to wire her $10,000. This was on a Sunday and I found out that they didn't wire money on Sundays in those days. I went out with Steve Rogers (Buck's son) and his wife. I was so hot that they wanted some of it to rub off on them. We lost Steve somewhere during the night and she and I went from casino to casino, winning. She ended up with $3,500. That streak was unbelievable! I played six hands of Blackjack at a time for $1,000 a hand. I owned the Craps tables. And I drew crowds of people wanting some of my luck to rub off on them. I got a little bothered by all of the attention and snuck across town from the Desert Inn, were I was staying, to another casino. I sat down at the bar and ordered a beer and the bartender said "Welcome, Mr. Runyon. The beer is on the house and we would love to have you play!" This was a bit of a surprise since I had never been in that particular spot before. The stick man at the craps table greeted me with "Hi, Larry, how are things in Kansas City?" This spooked me somewhat and when I got back to the Desert Inn I asked the General Manager, whom I had gotten to know, how somebody across town could know who I am and where I was from? He took me back to his office, typed in my name on a computer and up popped my name, date of birth, my job title, virtually everything about me! It turns out that if you win big or lose big in Vegas, they find out everything they can about you. As I said, I was 10 feet tall and bullet proof that week. Someone could have walked in firing an Uzi and he never would have grazed me! It all went well until the final couple of days of the conference. I went down to breakfast on the final day, a Sunday, and discovered that all I had was $20! I figured that I had somewhere in the neighborhood of $500,000 go into and out of my hands in the span of seven days! Buck Rogers joined me for breakfast and as he was commiserating with me over the down turn in my fortunes, I put my final $20 on a Keno card and it hits! When they came to deliver the money, Buck grabs it and sticks it in his pocket. He took it home and gave it to Sue. That $2,800 was all that I brought home out of all the winnings over a week's time!

Another time in Vegas I wasn't so lucky. My adverse fortune didn't have anything to do with gambling. I was at the Craps table and I was on a roll. Jack Klugman, the actor was standing next to me and betting right along with me. Soon he was up $25,000 and invited me for a drink. "You just made me the quickest $25,000 I ever made!" I went back to the tables and suddenly began hemorrhaging. I got up to my room, got the bleeding stopped and called Sue and had her get me an appointment with our doctor for the next day, I was taking the first plane home. They ran all kinds of tests and discovered that I had a tumor in my colon. Since it was right at the beginning of the golf season I asked if we could put it off until September. The doctor said no, it had to be done soon, like the next day! They referred me to a doctor who had developed a new method of operating on colon tumors. Dr. Tony Landers was a straight shooter as far as communicating with his patients was concerned. He told me that the tumor was one of the biggest he had ever seen. He explained that the traditional surgery would lay me up all summer but that his new method would have me back on my feet in a day or two. I said great, when do we start? He warned me of a few unusual factors with the new method. First, he told me, they couldn't give me any anesthetic. I asked if he realized that I was the biggest chicken alive? I couldn't even go to the dentist without breaking into a cold sweat! Dr. Landers told me not to worry, I would be fine. The next thing that I needed to know was that I needed to be awake because I had to help them with the operation! I was stunned and he took my hesitation for a positive response and booked an operating room for the next day. I watched on a small black and white screen as they threaded a wire loop up into my colon, set the loop around the tumor and tightened it. They then applied a charge and I could see the tumor go up in smoke. Since that time I have had seven more such operations, most by Dr. Landers. He advised me not to use any other doctor unless they had performed at least 400 of the procedures. I asked him how many he had performed when he did my first one. "Hell, Larry, you were the first son of a bitch I got to agree to it!"

While in South Africa I hired a guide to take me to Victoria Falls. I had read a great deal about Dr. Livingston who had discovered the falls in 1855. He described the rock formations that he saw around the falls and for years his notes never made any sense. The formations that he wrote of simply were not there! Then, just before I arrived, the rocks suddenly were visible. It seems that at the time that Dr. Livingston discovered them, there had been at least a six-year drought, just as there had been when I visited. The water level was low enough to reveal what the good doctor had seen.

When I got back from Africa I took a job at the Coronado Country Club back in El Paso, Texas. The course was located up on the side of the Franklin Mountains and was a pretty setting. The golf pro, Danny Swain, interviewed me for the job and he told me that the members liked fast greens. In fact, he said that there was no way that I could possibly make the greens too fast for them. After I had been there about a year they had a board meeting and Swain came to me and said, "Ahem. Is there any way that you can slow these greens down?" I had them running at an Augusta-like 13 on the step meter. We had a pro tournament about this time and the wind was really blowing. The pros would putt with a quarter in their hand and after they putted the ball they would run after it and mark it the instant that it stopped. Otherwise the wind would blow it completely off of the green! One of the pros, Jamie Crow, was asked who he thought would win the tournament. He said, "It won't be the best golfer. It will be the son of a bitch who can run fastest!"

Danny Swain is famous for other things besides hiring me as superintendent. He was a great storyteller, too. One of my favorites was about a friend of his who was a pro at a mid-western golf course that for obvious reasons will remain nameless. It seems that this guy attended a meeting of the PGA that centered on Women's Golf and ways of promoting it. He sat through a number of speakers and presentations and then someone gets up and tells the assembled attendees that there is a golf pro present that had one of the most successful ladies' golf programs in the country. They read his name and asked if he would mind standing up and explaining his enormously successful program. This golf pro stood up, in front of this entire audience who were there for only one reason...Ladies' Golf, and says, "I went to the Mid-West Country Club some twelve years ago. At that time we had 78 women golfers. I instituted my program and it has worked extremely well. I now have women's membership down to only 12!" Reportedly he got icy stares from the women and nervous laughter from the men. Some people just can't take a joke!

This is where I really got serious about using biological agents in sand greens to make them more efficient. During the five years that I was there I think I only sprayed the greens once for fungus. I became convinced that the use of biologicals was the preferred method of treatment on golf courses.

Coronado Country Club had one of the worst irrigation systems that I have ever seen. The pipes were rusted and there were leaks everywhere. There was one fairway residence that we flooded out four times! The last time I was walking up the front steps to talk to the owners and when they opened the door the wave of water knocked me off of my feet! The lady didn't speak English and I'm not sure what language she did speak but I could tell that she thought that it was my entire fault and I was being cussed out pretty good!

I seemed to have had water trouble a lot at Coronado. There was this big wedding and we set up a big circus tent alongside the eighth fairway. The place was all decked out with tables and chairs and decorations and this huge wedding cake. I had turned off the sprinklers for the duration of the ceremonies and reception. My assistant discovered them off and turned them back on. Just as the bride and groom were cutting the cake, up popped a big ol' sprinkler and started to soak everyone in the tent. People were running everywhere, looking to get away from the water. They were crashing into each other and the tables and the band. Everybody ended up with a piece of cake…somewhere on his or her body!

There are not many folks that I can't get along with but there was a retired general by the name of Cassidy on the board at Coronado that I just could not see eye to eye with. One of my major projects was to build walls around the course. About half way through the project the General became president of the board. He got to inspecting the walls and the balance sheet and said that there was no way that I was building them as cheap as I was. We got into a huge argument over it and I ended up quitting. Not long after I left and they hired a crew to come in and finish the walls, General Cassidy came to me and apologized. I've always admired him for that. They discovered that I had been using the maintenance workers and native rock from a nearby dry river bed and my only expense was for concrete. When they took out the labor expense for the crew that they hired they discovered that the price was exactly what I had been building them for. The general really is a good guy and I still see him from time to time.

Even though I was the superintendent I still kept my hand in teaching as much as I could. During a tournament one time I was helping a young pro by the name of Angus Baker polish his game and he said that he wanted me to come up to the driving range and see this friend of his hit some. It seemed that this friend was pushing the ball a bit and needed some help. I was introduced to this big, blonde kid who introduced himself as John Daly. I asked him to hit one for me and he did. I asked where it had gone because I never saw it leave the club head. Pretty soon I hear a "Bang!" I looked out at the range and asked John if that was his ball that just hit the roof of my maintenance shed. He said that it was. I asked him to hit another and the same thing happened. I figured that I had better help correct his "Push" or I might lose the maintenance shed! I made an adjustment to his shoulder position and he continued to send rockets out across the range that I never saw! Several years later I was out at the

Fairbanks Ranch Country Club in San Diego when the Walrus, Craig Stadler, was having his annual get together with the pros for junior Golf. I was standing by the twelfth fairway with a couple of guys and here comes John Daly. I told the guys that I had given John a couple of lessons a few years before. I won't say that they called me a liar, but they did scoff at the idea. They scoffed until John walked right up to me and said, "Runyon, what the hell are you doing here?" I was surprised that he remembered me after all that time and my companions were stunned!

Gene Fisher, the famous poker player, was a member at Coronado and I played many rounds with him. He once told me a story about playing in Las Vegas with Amarillo Slim, another famous poker player, Don Cherry, the singing golf pro and the fourth guy by the name of Leon who was a real long ball hitter. Leon had this guy with him that he called Squirrel that was backing all of his bets. He had been pounding the ball all day, especially the five woods which he put almost into orbit and far down the fairway. When they got to the 17th green, Gene asked him if he thought that he could hit one over the Hilton Hotel with his five wood. Leon said yes, he thought that he could hit a ball over the Hilton Hotel, which was adjacent to the green. Gene put up $10,000 that Leon couldn't do it. He was the only one to bet against Leon. Amarillo Slim didn't want in and Don Cherry wasn't much of a gambler, anyway. It was decided that Leon would have two shots to make one clear the hotel. Leon tees up the first ball and nails a drive that climbed and climbed and then went down like an elevator and landed on a sixth floor balcony! They later calculated that the ball would have to have traveled over 550 yards to have cleared the hotel. It also dawned on them that Leon might put one through a window of an occupied room. Leon put his 5 wood back in his bag and started back for the clubhouse. Squirrel asked him where he was going; he had another ball to hit. "No, I don't," he said, "I can't hit it any better than that!"

Gene Fisher was present at one of my more infamous moments, which happened several years later. We were going to go the track at Sunland

Park in El Paso. The track had initiated the double trifecta and it had been running all summer and nobody had hit it. It was up to $288,000 to the winner. I told Sue before I left the house that if I could get a winner in the first race, I just knew that the second race was going to be the 7-8-9 combination. Gene and I meet Hall of Fame basketball coach Don Haskins and his son Brent at the track. I had two winning tickets for the first race and there were only six winners out. When it came time to bet the second trifecta, I told my group that I was going to bet the 7-8-9. Coach Haskins tells me that I'd better talk to his son, Brent, because he has been winning and he has the scoop on who is going to win. I listened to him and thought about it and thought about it and just before post time I changed my bet to go with the coach's son. I know that you won't be too surprised to learn that the 7-8-9 combination came in and one other guy had it and walked away with $288,000! Afterward the coach and I were standing at the bar and I thought he was going to die! He felt so bad that I had lost out on all of that money. When I got home Sue had heard on the radio that the 7-8-9 combo had won and that there was one winning ticket in the double trifecta. Of course she was sure that the winner was me! It took me a while to explain what had happened and that I really hadn't bet the 7-8-9! Sue took it better than coach Haskins did, however. For over a year, every time he saw me he apologized and worried about losing $288,000 for me. I kept telling him not to worry about it and besides, it would only have been $144,000 since I would have had to split it with the other ticket holder, so it was no big deal! I have a lot of admiration for coach Haskins and his family. So much so that I have worked with the coach's other son, Steve, who is an extremely gifted golfer who is now on the Nike tour. I just don't ask any of them for tips at the track!

There is a story about Steve and his roommate, J.P. Hayes that is told around the circuit. It seems that the two of them were to play in the Nike Bakersfield tournament and I decided to go up and watch them. After the first round I went back up to their room on the second floor for a Budweiser or three. Their room looked out over the parking lot to the driving range. The room didn't have sliding doors out to the balcony; it had big, wide, swinging doors. These guys had been hitting balls out of the room, through the doors, over the parking lot and onto the driving range. When I got there they asked me if I'd like to hit one. I said sure, hand me a club. J.P. handed me his eight iron and I threw down a ball and sized up the shot. I noted where the TV was and where the table and chairs were positioned. I also took note of Steve and J.P. sitting on the beds, watching TV. I addressed the ball and executed a perfect swing, hitting it dead square. The next thing I knew, there was something flying around the room! Steve and J.P. are diving under the beds and I'm looking for a place to hide, thinking that it is the ball that hit something in the room and is bouncing off of the walls! The problem was that it didn't sound exactly like a golf ball. That's when I looked down and saw that the head was missing from J.P.'s eight iron! All that I'm holding onto was the shaft! That eight iron head made about four trips around the room before it landed. It seems that I clipped the edge of a table with my follow through and sheared the head clean off. We never did find out if the ball made it to the driving range or not. Poor ol' J.P. was without an eight iron the rest of the tournament. I don't remember that it bothered much, though.

When it came time to leave Coronado Country Club I went to Odessa, Texas and the Mission Country Club. Sue and the kids stayed in El Paso and I got an apartment in Odessa. My job at Mission was the try to turn things around. The course had been built right at the height of the oil boom and the oil business had since gone bust. The idea was to get the course in tiptop shape so that the membership would increase. The club was so broke that it became obvious that bankruptcy was the only hope. In the meantime I couldn't cash my paychecks! I played a little poker in the men's locker room to help with expenses. I did that until the day I caught one of the boys cheating. That ended my Odessa poker days.

Odessa was a blue-collar town. If a person strikes it rich in oil they move over to Midland. The country around Odessa is as flat as a pancake. I believe that the sixteenth green at Mission Country Club is the highest point in the whole county! Another interesting feature is that there are oil wells everywhere. A whole forest of them. The richest oil basin in the United States lays beneath Odessa, Texas. When you fly over the area, you can go for an hour and see nothing but oil wells. The people are real nice, though. Except maybe for a few police officers.

One night about one o'clock in the morning I was sitting on the hood of my pickup truck waiting for the irrigation to cycle to the north end of the course to make sure that some repairs that we had made that day were working. Suddenly two Odessa police came roaring out there in their squad car, slid to a stop in front of me and jerked me off of the hood. They tore my left rotator cuff and dislocated my left thumb. They kept asking me what I was doing there and I kept asking them what they were doing there. It was an unsatisfactory conversation for all concerned. They handcuffed me, threw me in the back of their car and off to jail I went. They had asked me whose pick up I was sitting on and I told them it belonged the club. They ran the plates and found that it belonged to the leasing company that the club dealt with. They thought that it must be stolen. It wasn't until they started to book me that I found out that they thought that I was vandalizing the course. The Odessa cops were out of their jurisdiction. They handled the streets but the course came under the Sheriff's duties. After I got things squared away, I filed a suit against the Odessa police for $1,000,000. My attorneys and I knew that we had them nailed. However a couple of the cops pulled me aside one day and told me that if I didn't drop the suit, it was just a matter of time before they had my driver's license and I would never get it back. From then on, every time I left the gates of the club, I'd see an Odessa cop in my rear view mirror. When they couldn't get me, they started nailing the members as they came out. Finally the club president came to me and said, "Runyon, if you don't drop this lawsuit, there isn't going to be a member out here with a driver's license!" I reluctantly dropped the suit the next day.

On Friday nights I would drive home to El Paso to see Sue and the kids. Every time I would pass a sign that read "Wink, Texas 11 miles." The first Friday after Roy Orbison, the great singer, passed away I took that turnoff and visited the town where he went to high school. When Roy was living there it was a staging area for the bombers during WWII and had a population of about 25,000. Today you'd have to count everybody twice to get 800! I pulled into a diner and ordered a cup of coffee from this ol' gal and asked her if she had known Roy Orbison. "I surely did," she drawled, "I went to high school with him." I asked if he sang back then. "He surely did. There wasn't much to do except fight, fuck or sing!" She got right up in my face and said, "Myself, I couldn't sing a lick!"

Wink didn't have much on Odessa as far as small towns were concerned. High school football was king in Odessa. They have a tremendous program that churns out championship teams year after year. The fans are fanatical and have built a world-class stadium for the team to play in. You've got to understand that there really is nothing else to do in Odessa except watch football and the paint dry! To show you how rabid the fans were, I was playing golf with some local businessmen one day and one of them mentioned that he heard that old Billy Bob had died the night before. The other two hadn't heard but one of them said that at the turn he was going to call the widow and give his condolences. I asked why the hurry and he said that Billy Bob had great seats at the high school stadium, better than his and if he acted quickly enough he might be able to buy them. He came back and joined us on the tenth tee. I asked him how it went and he said that he had given her his condolences and then asked if she might want to sell Billy Bob's tickets. She told him that he was too late; she had already sold them to the mortician!

There is one guy who will never be able to show his face in Odessa again. He is the one who wrote the book about Odessa football called *Saturday Night Lites*. It wasn't exactly complimentary about the town, its people or its football program. He revealed the regular practice of recruiting violations, illegal practices, gambling and obsessive/compulsive parents. The Chamber of Commerce won't soon be handing him a Good Citizen plaque!

I won't say that Odessans are off beat, but they are a might eccentric! I was hunting quail with a friend of mine and we were hunting the canyons outside of town. The sportsmen in Odessa, Texas hunt their quail from a jeep. We were driving along, looking for our next quail and this ol' boy slams on the brakes. I didn't know what was going on, whether we ran over something or a quail was charging the jeep or what. This guy jumps out, pops the hood and pulls out a long package covered in aluminum foil. He lays it on the hood, unwraps it and announces that lunch was served! He had mashed potatoes and gravy, pork chops and corn, all heated by the manifold of that old jeep! I'm not saying that it wasn't a good idea, mind you; it was just a little strange!

The financial situation was so bad at Mission Country Club that I decided that I couldn't wait around for another oil boom, so I took a job with Karsten Solhiem at Ping Golf in Phoenix, Arizona. Karsten had lived on the Moon Valley Country Club for many years and when it hit hard times and went bankrupt Karsten took it over. After he had been there awhile he became very alarmed at the amount of chemicals that were being used to maintain the golf course. He launched a program to not necessarily eliminate chemicals but at least use less of them. At the same time Karsten became aware of a machine that was being used in the cattle industry to test feed in cattle feedlots. Dr. Shank at Penn State University had developed it. He had developed the machine to test for proteins in the cattle feed. It was based on near infrared spectroscopy and Karsten thought that maybe that machine could be taught to read turf grass. I was hired to come in and help develop the machine because by that time I had a reputation for maintaining golf courses using less and less chemicals. I worked for about a year with a group that Karsten put together and we finally did build a machine that would test turf grass for various nutrients. The Ping people wanted to sell a machine to each golf course while my idea was to install a machine in a mobile lab and take it from course to course.

While I worked for Ping I was living in a house owned by Allan Solhiem, Karsten's son. In the garage of this house was a very rare Ford

Mustang, which had the biggest engine ever, put into a Mustang? Very few of them were ever built. Karsten had purchased the car for Alan to drive at 100MPH while Karsten held a golf club, with ribbons tied to the head, out of the window to observe airflow. Actually, Alan said that most of the trips were above 100MPH since Karston kept telling him to go a little faster. This obviously was prior to Ping getting a wind tunnel.

The Solhiem family was a real nice group of people. I had a lot of fun working there. They were also a very religious family. Each Thursday morning they would have a prayer meeting in the clubhouse. They would open up the sliding walls that encompassed the bar area and the dining room. There usually would be somebody famous that would speak and a big crowd always showed up. Every now and then a member would come in from an early round and say in a loud voice, expecting the bartender to be there, "I'll have a double Scotch on the rocks!" He then would look around and discover that he was in the middle of a prayer meeting. It was usually enough to put him on the wagon for a while!

After the machine was developed and ready for the market, I heard from a friend of mine who was a member at the Coronado Country Club in El Paso, as well as at Rancho Santa Fe, about an opportunity that presented itself at Rancho Santa Fe Country Club in San Diego, California. They had been looking for someone to rebuild the course for about four years. They were looking for someone who had building experience so I went over and interviewed for the job and came back to Ping. A few days later I got a phone call that Rancho Santa Fe had narrowed their search down to three people. They wanted me to write down what I would do if I were hired to take over the responsibilities of rebuilding the course. I figured that the other two guys would tell how short they would cut the grass and how many times a year they would aerate the greens and so on. I sat down and wrote a letter in which I told them that I thought that Rancho Santa Fe Golf Club was like a rare antique that had been setting up in the barn for a number of years. It should be brought down, cleaned up and polished every day, and displayed proudly in the front room. They called me a couple of days later and told me I had the job.

Rancho Santa Fe is one of the wealthiest clubs in the United States. Bing Crosby started his famous "Clam Bake" Pro/Am tournament there in 1934 before moving after WWII to Pebble Beach. There were many beautiful houses along the fairways and it seemed that there was a story with each one of them. For instance I hired a guy by the name of Cope to handle the bookkeeping and record keeping while I was there. He did a fine job and was a real nice guy. One day I came into the office and said that he wouldn't believe what they were doing to that big ol' house across from the 5th green. He asked what that might be. I told him that they were bulldozing it into rubble. Cope said he'd like to see that and we jumped into the pickup. I told him on the way over that I had asked why they were tearing down such a beautiful home and they said that it was beautiful on the outside but ugly on the inside. I asked what they meant and they told me that whoever had designed the house had no idea of what they were doing, it was just terrible. When we got to the house a bulldozer was pushing over walls and the house was collapsing on itself. I looked over at Cope and he had tears in his eyes. He told me that was his house, that he was the one who had designed it. It turns out that he had grown up in Bing Crosby's house and had designed this one. He had gone to Saudi Arabia and lost the family fortune and had to sell the house.

My job at Rancho Santa Fe was to rebuild all of the greens, tee boxes and sand traps, put in a new irrigation system, replant all of the fairways, build all new bridges and bury some high-power lines across two fairways. All of this and I had eleven months to do it! And I couldn't close one day! Not one hole could be closed for even a part of one day! We finished the job in ten months and there never was a time when all 18 holes were not in play. I won't say that there was pressure, but the job started out as a six-pack of Bud per day endeavor and ended up as a 16 Bud per day job!

It took an unbelievably strong and competent board to undertake that project. The driving force behind the project was a gentleman by the name of Stewart Bowie. After I met with him he went back to the board and told them that he thought that they had found someone with enough experience and dumb enough to take on their project!

So we got started and things were going well. About halfway through I was flagged down by this old gentleman who lived over on the front nine. He wanted to know how long things were going to be torn up. I was feeling pretty good about the situation and told him we ought to be through in about ten months, a month early. It shouldn't be long at all, I told him. "Kiddo, at my age I don't even buy green bananas!" He was still kicking when the job was done.

That project was an extremely interesting one. There was a lot of history in that course. When we redid the ninth green we found three other greens underneath. The greens chairman paid us a visit just as we were starting to dig and told us that we would find a USGA green under the existing one. He said that he knew this because he had been greens chairman when it was built. I asked what happened and he said that they had used muck soil turf and it had never worked out so they built the present one on top of it. Sure enough, we found the USGA green and the one that they had built that on top of.

I had an interesting visitor every day. Victor Mature, the great actor, lived across the street from the club and would stop by every day to see how things were going. He used to drive Chuck Courtney, the head pro, crazy. Victor had a red golf cart with a fireman's hat with a red light on top mounted on the front. He had a portable stereo system that he played classical music on while he played golf. He had a set of barbells in the cart that he would use to work out between shots. He just drove everybody crazy. He never teed up with anyone; he would just cut in at some hole, hit four or five shots and go to another hole. He was in great shape back then and played every day, as he had since he moved into his house across the street in 1941. I was having a beer at a place called Quimby's with Victor on his

74th birthday. That was when I experienced my first earthquake. We were sitting and talking over matters of great importance when the chandeliers started to sway, the glasses behind the bar started to rattle and the floor started to move. Victor looks at me and says "Kid, get ready, we're having a shaker!" With that he took along draw on his beer and we waited it out.

Rancho Santa Fe Golf Club is located in one of the prettiest little villages you could imagine. It has Great restaurants, shops and services and really nice people. It also has some of the nicest year around weather of any place in the country. I stayed in a member's guesthouse for a while when I first arrived and got to know the town pretty well. After a few months my son Larry moved out and we got an apartment in Vista, up the road from Rancho Santa Fe.

Chuck Courtney, the head pro at the club, became a good friend of mine. He had been on the pro tour for about 12 years and was a good teaching pro. We were discussing boards of directors one night over a beer or two and I told him that it had been my observation that the worst board members were doctors and lawyers. "If you can keep them off of the board," I said, "You're much better off." It wasn't until a year later that I found out that his dad was a dentist! Now I should say right here that even though my observations about board members are fairly accurate, there are exceptions. My attorney, for instance, is a board member and Greens Chairman at a club and he serves the membership well.

Even though I rebuilt the course from stem to stern there are 3 greens that I don't ever want my name connected with! Number 17, 18 and 3 are absolutely "Committee Greens." Especially the number three green. The greens committee decided that they simply had to get involved once it was obvious that the project was going to be done on time and at budget. I told the greens chairman, a man by the name of Ken Swanson (a real good guy), that he had to let me bulldoze the whole thing flat and start over. I said that I was going to be gone and he would have to live with it. The committee decided to keep it. It was a monstrosity! It had a valley in the middle that made putting an adventure. It was butt ugly! It was truly a committee green.

Rancho Santa Fe is one of the finest layouts that I have ever been on. Years ago they asked Sam Snead to pick his favorite 18 holes from around the country. Number 16 at Rancho Santa Fe was one that he chose. Because of the history of the course and because it was so beautiful, we tried to rebuild it as close to what it was originally as possible. I did a lot of research in the archives of the San Diego Library and found a bunch of pictures of the original Bing Crosby Clam Bake. We used these pictures to rebuild the greens to the way that they were. All, that is, except #3, #17 and #18. The greens committee built those. I had nothing to do with them!

When I first arrived at the course, southern California was in the midst of a four-year drought and I couldn't do any watering until 6 o'clock in the evening. That made the job twice as hard as it should have been. Rancho Santa Fe was the first course where I put biological agents in the greens construction. The result was that we had sixteen-inch roots in about six weeks. This was about double what would normally be expected. Deeper roots meant less down time, which meant members could use the new greens sooner.

By this time I was very much involved in achieving an important ambition of mine to develop a true Integrated Pest Management (IPM) program that would make the biological compatible with the chemical. It would not necessarily eliminate the chemical but remove the dependency on chemicals. I foresee a time when we have a combination of biologicals and chemicals that allows us to use less dangerous chemicals with a shorter residual.

Chapter 12

(Rancho Santa Fe was a very important stop on my grand tour of golf courses. First it established me in the highest echelons, pay scale wise, of Golf Course Superintendents. I had come a long way from a one man, $200 a month operation. My name was being mentioned in some pretty fancy circles as a guy who knew a lot about organics and turf grass maintenance. That leads me to the second reason that Rancho Santa Fe was so important.

About that time a guy by the name of Bill Adams was looking for something innovative in the golf industry. It seems that he and his partner, Jeff Johnson, had just taken a company public and had made a tidy sum. They had found another company, Eco Soil Systems, in Nebraska that was in trouble. Eco Soil Systems was dealing in specialized fertilizer formulations. Bill decided to buy the company and then go out and search for new ideas to get it turned around. He made a tour of the golf industry, asking if anyone had any new ideas that his company could develop. Most places he went he heard my name. One day Bill and Jeff showed up at my office at Rancho Santa Fe and explained what they had in mind and asked me what I thought about the Eco Soil Systems formulations. I told them that they would probably grow pretty good turf, but they wouldn't make any money. I told them that I had something out in the shop that might interest them. I took them to where I was brewing some microbes to use in the greens construction. I told them that I thought that I could eventually build a machine that would breed these microbes and inject them into the irrigation system and there would be a lot of benefits. I also had the Karsten/NIR computer that we had developed when I was at Ping to analyze the grass clippings for nutrients. My idea was to put the computer into a mobile laboratory. Bill came back to me about three days later with a complete business plan and offered me an opportunity to prove some of my theories. When I finished my work at Rancho Santa Fe we immediately began construction on what was to become known as a bioreactor and a system that would inject the microbes into the irrigation system.

This seems like a pretty good place to wax philosophically about education and its role in our society. There will be a lot of folks who will disagree with what I am about to say, but I believe that we put way too much emphasis on theory and book learning and not nearly enough on lessons learned from doing. In my travels with Eco Soils I have encountered what I have come to refer to as educational snobs. These are folks who peer down their nose at anyone who doesn't have an alphabet behind their name. They are also the same people who give immediate credence to anything uttered by someone who calls him or herself Doctor. I remember talking to one ol' boy at a trade show who was just in rapture over what I was telling him about microbial action as it pertained to turf management. I mean he was glowing at the possibilities that this afforded the golf course industry and was marveling at how much it was going to reduce the use of harmful chemicals. It was about this time that he asked me where I had gotten my PhD. "On the golf course," I told him. He kind of chuckled and said, "No, really." "Really. The last classroom I was in was in Sedan, Kansas." This ol' slick lost interest in me faster than if he was a Cadillac salesman who just found out I hadn't a dime to my name! I think that this epitomizes one of the major problems that we have in this country. We are losing faith in what used to be called "Good old Yankee know how". For over 200 years this country has benefited from people on farms and in workshops and garages who didn't have much of a formal education, but figured out how to make things run better or more productive or more economically just by native intelligence and the desire to make it happen.

Another thing that we have lost sight of is the value of apprenticeship. We have somehow come to believe that the only jobs worth having are those that require a college education or even higher education. If you give a kid the right atmosphere, the right encouragement and a good example, it is amazing what he can figure out on his own. Now, don't get me wrong. I'm not saying that nobody should go to college. Far from it. I am only suggesting that there are a lot of kids who get discouraged in the classroom and then get into all kinds of problems when they have no alternatives. On the job training could go a long way to keep kids productive and useful to themselves and their community. Everything that I know about turf and microbes and chemicals I learned by observation, trial and error and hard work. I don't know much about the "scientific method" but I know the power of "Tryin'". In other words, if you have a problem with the way something is working, try something else. We are so reluctant in this country to try anything until some old codger who has read 300 books about photosynthesis and osmosis and capillary attraction, but hasn't watered his own lawn in five years, puts his blessing on the latest "miracle" product to green up a lawn. In the meantime some wiseass like me is out coming up with "Cow Manure Tea" and making the country club set salivate over the turf on the fairways and greens.

All I'm saying is that we need to help our kids succeed by paying attention to what they are good at and help them. If he is a wiz at math and can do calculus in his head, by all means, keep him at, even if it leads to a PhD! But on the other hand, if she has no use for books, but loves to tinker in the garage and can tune your SUV to get 30 miles to the gallon, then please encourage her to apprentice with the best mechanic that you can find. And give her my address...I only get about 11 MPG.

The third reason that I think kindly of Rancho Santa Fe is a gentleman named Edward Ford. Mr. Ford was friends with a good many members and was a pretty good golfer. He and I shared a lemonade or two now and then and he became interested in my microbial ideas. When Bill, Jeff and I started working on the bioreactor, Mr. Ford was one of the first investors. That is how I came to know one of the greatest pitchers in baseball history, New York Yankee left hander, Whitey Ford. Whitey is a member of the Hall of Fame, had a lifetime record of 236 wins and 109 losses, a .690 winning percentage (third best of all time), broke Babe Ruth's

World Series record for consecutive scoreless innings pitched (Whitey had 32 to the Babe's 29) and he holds 8 World Series records. I found that everywhere I went, people knew Whitey Ford, even my mother, who was not a sports fan normally, was a huge Whitey Ford fan. I told my wife recently that as a young man I remembered watching Whitey pitch in the World Series a if anyone had told me that someday I would get to know him quite well, I'd have asked "How? I don't play baseball." That's one of the many times in my life that I realized what a great equalizer the game of golf is. I guess one of my biggest joys to come out of golf is my acquaintance with Whitey, a real character.

We were in Phoenix, Arizona one time, getting ready to get on a plane. As we approached the security gate, Whitey nudged me and said, "Watch this!" As he passed through the metal detector all of the bells and whistles went crazy. They asked him to go through again and once again the alarms sounded. He looked over at me and winked, walked through again and set the bells to ringing again. Finally, Whitey pulls out his wallet and shows them a card that states that Whitey Ford has a Titanium hip, a Titanium shoulder and various other metal apparatus that would surely give airport metal detectors fits. The action drew a crowd and it was amazing how quickly word spread that Whitey Ford was in the area. Whitey informed his adoring fans that "One more shoulder and I will be the bionic man!"

It is amazing to me that even the youngest generation knows who Whitey Ford is. People who were never Yankee fans respect and admire him. Everywhere we go, fans approach him for an autograph or just to say "Hi." To give you an idea of how far reaching his popularity and fame reaches, I was doing some work in Las Moches, Mexico in the agricultural industry and I was telling Whitey about it over drinks one evening. He told me that he had played with the team in Cuocan, Mexico and had played some games in Las Moches in 1945 or 1946. He had good memories of that time. I knew that there were many baseball fans in Las Moches and I asked him to sign some balls to take down with me. There are some very wealthy farmers down there and I don't think I could have made them happier if I had handed them a bar of gold! They asked if I could impose on Whitey to come down and throw out the first pitch at the start of the season. I assured them that my close personal relationship with the great man would insure his presence! When I got home I asked Whitey if he would be interested in flying down for the start of the Winter League and throwing out the first pitch. To my great relief, he said that he would LOVE to do that. We met in San Diego and along with Bill Adams and several members of the Eco Soils Board of Directors, drove across the border to Tijuana and boarded an Aero Mexico flight. On the way down Whitey and I sample a few snifters just to keep hydrated and we were met by this large contingent of civic leaders, business leaders and just plain baseball fans...everyone knows Whitey Ford. Now, Whitey is expecting to throw out the first pitch, watch the game and head back home. We went from the airport to the best restaurant in town and have a wonderful meal and a few more snifters. We headed for the ballpark in 100-degree heat with 100% humidity. When we got there the place was packed...standing room only! There are flags flying and bunting draped on the stands and dignitaries out on the field. It looked for all the world like the World Series. Bill Adams and Whitey head out to the mound and I'm watching all of this from the dugout. First there were speeches by the Mayor and the Baseball Commissioner and old time Mexican ballplayers. I'm watching Whitey and he is looking very uncomfortable about this time, but I figure when the speeches are over, he'll toss the ball and that will be it. As soon as the last speech is through, the local high school band marches onto the field and starts playing. Whitey is looking more and more uncomfortable in the heat and humidity. After about a half hour of band music, the cheerleaders appear from under the stands and begin to tumble and flip flop run all over the field. I can't tell from my vantage point whether Whitey is just pissed off or whether he is as uncomfortable as he looks. When the cheerleaders finally flipped their last flop and we all expected to see the Great Yankee pitcher deliver the first pitch, the

Mayor starts introducing the dignitaries from the audience! This went on seemingly forever and Whitey is looking worse and worse. Just when we figured that all of the pomp and circumstance was over, we hear an explosion and the fireworks started. The only problem was that the first one, which was designed to go 300-400 feet in the air, decided to make a right hand turn and shoot across the field at a height of about 6 feet! It glanced off of one of the dignitaries and exploded along the third base line. I figured that, man, that was the end of the fireworks, now we can get Whitey off the field. How wrong I was! They shot off, by my actual count, fifteen of those suckers and not ONE of them went any higher than 6 feet and they all bounced around the field and into the stands. People were diving for cover under the stands, out in the parking lot, anywhere they could find cover. At one point I looked out at the mound and Whitey was spread eagled on the ground with his hands covering his head. When order was finally restored, Whitey fired a strike to the catcher, waved to the crowd and headed for the dugout. I saw his problem right away, he was totally dehydrated for the 100 plus degree heat and the extreme humidity. We decided that Whitey had to get back to the motel and get some water into him. As we started to leave, we heard sirens and there is a big commotion out in the parking lot. It seems that a house was on fire and the fire trucks were laying hoses all over the place! It took some creative driving, but we finally got out of there and back to the motel. Bill and the others decided that I would stay with Whitey and they would return to the field and cover the rest of the activities. Just before they left, Bill reminds me that there were 65 baseballs that Whitey was to sign for all of the dignitaries. Now here the guy is, almost passed out of heat exhaustion and I'm supposed to ask him to sign 65 balls! The first thing that I did was order all of the bottled water I could lay my hands on. Whitey was drinking with both fists and starting to feel a little better. I knew he was feeling better when he said, "I suppose the next Goddamn thing you want me to do is sign a bunch of baseballs!" I said, "Only 65." He told me to lay them out on the bed the next morning and he would come by at 5:30 and sign them all. And he did! I took him to the airport and he flew to New York where he was to sit in George Stienbrenner's box at the World Series. Now he still wasn't looking real good, but he was better than when he was spread eagled on the mound in Las Moches! A couple of days later I called to see how he was doing and they told me that he had had brain surgery. I called the next day and they said that he was doing fine, it was non-cancerous and the prognosis was good. The next day I called and they had got him back in surgery and put a pace maker in his heart! I figured it was one more thing to set off the airport alarms! I talked to him shortly thereafter and he said, "Runyon, you almost killed me! But you saved my life so we're still friends!" I'm glad that we are. Whitey Ford is one of the most genuinely nice people I have ever met. He has been on the Board of Directors for Eco Soils for several years and he has appeared at trade shows and signed balls and talked with fans for hours without ever complaining. Yes, Eco Soils has opened a lot of doors for me.

I almost didn't live to see all of this come to pass. I was living just north of San Diego at the time and had discovered the greatest hamburger stand I have ever eaten at. It was called the Nessie Burger and was owned by a Scotsman who had grown up on the shores of Loch Ness in Scotland. It was my habit to stop there most mornings and have a Nessie Burger for breakfast. I had had my usual burger this one morning and I was on the freeway, headed for work when I got to feeling pretty bad. I had this strange feeling in my chest and I suspected that I might be having a heart attack. I pulled over and got out of the car and took some deep breaths and pulled myself together and started to feel a little better. I went on into the office, still feeling kind of rocky, but better than I had. After lunch I got to feeling bad again and left for the day. When I got home I asked Sue to drive me to the hospital because I suspected that I might have had a heart attack. They ran all sorts of tests and came to the conclusion that I probably did have a heart attack. Because I was in pretty good shape they felt that I should have an Angioplasty, were they slip a tube into your artery and expand a balloon wherever there is a blockage. As I was on the operating table, the doctor tells me that Angioplasty isn't going to work, that I needed a bypass operation. I told him to go ahead and do it. I thought that they could do it right then. It turned out to be the next day.

A doctor came in to interview me and asked me to lay out all of my habits for the past two months, especially anything different. I went through my eating habits and my exercise habits and told him that the only thing that I had done out of the ordinary had been to quit drinking beer about six weeks before. He asked how much I had been drinking and I told him I would come home from work and have a few beers. He said, "That's it! The beer was thinning out your blood so that it passed through the blockages without producing any pain." I said, "OK, bring me a six pack and cancel the operation!" He thought that was pretty funny but wouldn't write me a prescription. I had a quadruple bypass the next morning. I felt better for a while after the operation and then started to feel bad again. I considered retiring about that time and we had bought a place in Las Cruces, New Mexico. When I took my prescriptions to my new pharmacy the pharmacist looked at them and asked me how I felt. I said that I felt terrible. He asked me if it was all right to call my doctor out in California because something didn't look right. When he got off the phone he told me that I was taking twice as much medication as I should be! Within four days I was feeling great and thinking of going back to work.

Anyway, before all of that happened I applied for the first patents on the machine and the delivery system. Everyone told me that I didn't have an ice cube's chance in hell of getting a dual patent like that. I seemed to be the only one who wasn't concerned. Sure enough, a year later we received the first two patents and since then we have added five more for a total of seven patents on the process. We also have approval from the Environmental Protection Agency (EPA). During this time we had installed the very first bioreactor at Bonita Golf Club, just east of San Diego, California. Things went so well that the Crockett family, who owns the course, became the first investors in Eco Soil Systems. I might mention that Bob Scribner, the Superintendent at Bonita was very helpful in getting things started there. Next we went to Fairbanks Ranch Country Club where they were contemplating the installation of a $1,000,000 desalinization plant to treat the irrigation water. Some of the board members there had heard of what we were doing and were very interested. It was not unanimous, however. The board was split almost down the middle as to which remedy they wanted. It just so happened that Gene Littler, the great touring pro, was a member of the board at the time. He liked what we were doing and he championed our cause. It is not an over statement to say that he was instrumental in the board approving our installation. The Superintendent was Brian Derrick and he was really high on our process, along with the Greens Chairman, Glenn Evans. We hooked up a separate irrigation line to one of the greens and decided to run it for a year using the bioreactor. After only a few months the difference was so dramatic that the test was abandoned and the system was installed on the entire course. They never did have to install the desalinization plant. The micro organisms that we used were high polysaccharide producers which aggregated the soil and allowed it to drain, hence the salt would flush out and not cause a caustic build up.

Since that time we have discovered that several universities have been researching the use of microorganisms but have been unable to make them work outside of the laboratory. I had heard about a Dr. John Menge from the University of California Riverside who was trying to take a microorganism from the lab to the field to fight phytophora root rot disease in avocado and citrus. I made an appointment to see him and showed him what we were doing with our machine and he immediately recognized it as the answer to his problem. Once we had made the connection with Dr. Menge we were able to associate ourselves with 4 other major universities. Once we teamed up with some of them we started to see unbelievable success. This success, I believe, will revolutionize the golf maintenance industry. It will also, I believe, revolutionize the agricultural industry. There is a fairly long list of chemicals that are used all over the world that face a deadline for termination in the year 2001. There have been no acceptable alternatives yet, but we think the biologicals will fill the gap. I also believe we will develop a system to solve one of the biggest problems facing mankind...water pollution.

Most people don't realize that there is only a finite amount of water in this ol' world. It collects in depressions, evaporates and falls as rain. New water is not being manufactured. However, existing water is being polluted at an alarming rate. The biggest culprit is nitrates, which leach into the water table from fertilizers and other toxins. The problem is not necessarily the over use of chemical fertilizers, it is the sterilization of the microbial population, which interrupts the natural cycle in the soil. I believe that we can clean up nitrate-leaden water with a microbial process that will turn the nitrates into proteins. What we are really doing is restoring the natural balance. Eco Soils is working on such a system and it should be ready in the near future.

Some of the first investors in Eco Soil Systems were professional golfers. Their interest stems from the fact that they spend an enormous amount of time on the turf that has been laden with all of these chemicals that get absorbed in the leather soles of their shoes and eventually into their feet. They were and are excited to find something that maintains good turf and uses fewer chemicals.

There have been some interesting conversations with folks about what these microorganisms are and what they do. I remember one superintendent asking how many we intended to put on his course. I told him there would be about a billion or two sprayed out from the bioreactor and through the irrigation system. "Well, how big do they get?" he wanted to know. I told him we weren't quite sure, but the biggest we had seen was no bigger than Mickey Rooney! He had a hell of a time trying to figure out where all of those Mickey Rooneys were going to stand and not interfere with the golf. He finally figured out that I must have been pulling his leg.

When we first started out, Bill Adams and I would call on the golf course superintendents together. Now Bill had not spent much time around the maintenance part of golf courses and so I took the first few presentations to give him a feel for it. He told me after the first few that I was doing a good job but I was using the word "I" too often. A couple of weeks later we decided that Bill was ready to take the lead on a presentation and he did. Afterwards, he asked how he had done. I told that he had done a good job, but he used the word "I" twenty-one times!

At one the next presentations, someone asked how safe these microbes were. Now the answer is that microorganisms are basically harmless when applied to the turf or anything agricultural, but Bill decided that he wanted to take it one step further. "I'll tell you how safe they are. I'd eat them on my Post Toasties!" We had a sample of the microbes in a bag and they scrambled all over the clubhouse kitchen looking for Post Toasties. Luckily, they never found any. I don't know what the reaction would be if these things were ingested prior to being brewed in the bioreactor, but I wasn't ready to find out. When we got out to the parking lot I asked Bill what he would have done if they had handed him a bowl of Post Toastics. "I had it all figured out," he said, "I was going to push the bowl in front of you and say 'Here, Larry, you haven't had breakfast yet, you have them!'"

I've been fortunate enough to travel to places that as a kid with polio, back in Sedan, Kansas, I never dreamed I would see. One country that I have enjoyed visiting is Mexico. We have been doing some work with the agricultural authorities down there using soil inoculants. We have one that, in its early stages, competes for the same food source as the soil pathenigens. When the inoculant dies, its' carcass turns into an antibiotic. We've got them coming and going!

Microorganisms have been around forever; it is just that nobody has been able to figure out how to make them work. There have been academic types working on the project for a good many years. Now I'm just a poor ol' country boy from the dusty Kansas plains, with a degree from the University of Hard Knocks and a pretty good dose of common sense.

Some of the Master's degrees and PhD's just can't quite bring themselves to come out and say that I was the one that invented the successful process. Most of them will tell you that they knew about it all along, but they were too busy to file for the patent! I have found that the very educated have learned out of a book and are extremely linear thinkers. A guy like me drives these guys nuts! One of them asked one time at Eco Soil Systems what kind of degree did I have? I told them that I didn't have a degree, but I had a bunch of them working for me! I have found that most academic types first try to figure out why something won't work. They are the most negative thinkers that I have ever seen. I don't have the burden of an education and, not knowing any better, I try to figure out ways to make things work.

There is justice in this world, I have discovered. Recently I traveled to Korea to deliver a talk about our work at Eco Soil Systems and when I arrived I found that my name in the program and on my name badge was preceded by "Dr." I have gotten some mileage out of that, believe you me.

As I said, my work with Eco Soil Systems has taken me literally all over the world. One spot, in particular, sticks out in my mind. One day just before I finished Rancho Santa Fe I got a visit from a big ol' ex-football lineman by the name of Chuck Fox. It seems that he was importing some peat moss from Ireland. This peat was much richer than the Canadian stuff that we had been using and I found that it was a much better product to use as an organic base for our microorganisms. When we started Eco Soil Systems, I called Chuck and he suggested that we go over to Ireland and see how the peat is harvested and talk to their experts about what I was doing. When we got there the Irish Peat Authority, Bord Na Mona, were wonderful hosts. Joe Whittle was our chief guide and companion during our trip and we visited some great pubs as well as the bogs and processing plant. We also met with the marketing director of Bord Na Mona, Herman Mulder. Now Herman was a Dutchman who lived in France and worked for the Bord in Ireland. He decided to drive us from Dublin to the bogs in Port Laois, about a hundred miles or so southwest.

We were cruising along the N7 highway, talking about turf and golf and peat, and doing about eighty miles an hour. I was sitting in the back seat and Chuck was in the front seat with Herman driving. I should point out that they drive on the wrong side of the road over there and it takes some getting used to. Just watching them drive like that puts a body in the first stages of fright. So here we are, screaming down the highway with all of these cars coming at us on the right, no divider between us, and Herman is trying to keep the conversation going about importing peat into the United States. Herman's only problem was that he has a habit of looking directly at the person he is talking to, even while driving and even if the person is in the back seat! Now Chuck and I are keeping a keen eye on the oncoming traffic and I suddenly realize that Herman isn't! He's turned around making some point about the peat and I can see that we are drifting toward the oncoming lane, headed right for another car coming the other way. I know that Chuck sees it, too, because he as twitchy as a whore in a Baptist church. I reached a point where I didn't know whether to holler or duck. I was afraid that if I hollered, Herman might jerk the wheel even further to the right. Chuck gasped and was reaching for the wheel just as Herman calmly turned around and straightened out, missing the oncoming car by a whisker. I mean you couldn't have put a hand between the two cars! Joe Whittle and a couple of others were following us and when we stopped for lunch, Joe asked what was wrong with Chuck and I; we looked white as a ghost. He suggested that we needed a pint to calm the nerves. I don't think that I ever enjoyed a drink more in my life!

That was a very interesting trip for many reasons. First it was enlightening to see how the Irish harvest peat and the innovations that they have developed for delivery around the world. I remain convinced that theirs is a superior product if they can only figure out how to get into this country at an acceptable price. They're working on it.

I learned something about Irish course maintenance and how it sheds light on the history of the old west in America. We were invited to play golf at a very unique course that used to be an artillery practice range when the British Army was stationed in Ireland. It's called the Curragh and is across the highway from where they run the Irish Sweepstakes horse race. The traps on the course are big, deep grass bunkers with sand at the very bottom. Another interesting feature was that all of the turf was the same height; there was no rough at all. We got to the third hole and I looked down the fairway and there was a flock of sheep out in the middle. I asked Des O'Brien, our host and the Greens Chairman, what that was all about and he told me that the sheep kept the grass clipped down to a uniform length. I wondered how that could be since I knew that there had been huge range wars in the West over sheep ruining the cattle feed because they ate the grass right down to the roots. Besides that I wondered how they kept the sheep off the greens. Des told me that the grass on the greens was too short for them to eat. "But, Des," I said, "Sheep in the old west ate right down to the roots!" "Ah, now, Laddie," Des says, "You Americans obviously don't know the first thing about sheep. You must have imported the kind with thin lips!" I found this rather hard to believe until he showed me the thick lips on their sheep and they were as thick as the grass was tall! When I got home I went the local county fair and made a beeline for the sheep pens. Sure enough, there were the thinnest lipped sheep I had ever seen. Imagine how different the west would have been if they had the thick lipped sheep! Of all of the countries that I have visited, none are more friendly or nicer than the Irish. It is a lovely country, but it will scare the wits out of you on the highways!

As I said, Eco Soil Systems has taken me to places that I never thought I'd go. Another prime example of this is the Pauma Valley Country Club. This is a course that used to be on the Top 100 list. It has an impressive membership list and is really difficult to get into. One day Bill Adams came to me and told me that he thought that it was time for me to look at the other side of golf. He suggested that I put in a membership application at Pauma Valley and look around the area for a house that Sue and I might like to live in. "Go live the good life," he told me, "Find out how the other half lives!" That sounded pretty good to me, so I applied for membership and found a house that we would move into for the 41st move of our married life.

I found out that there was a lot of history connected with the Pauma Valley Country Club. It turned out that the acreage once belonged to John Wayne. During WWII the Duke decided that there was a better than even chance that the U.S. would be invaded by the Japanese. He looked around for someplace inland from his Newport Beach, California home and found the ranch in Pauma Valley. He built a beautiful log home and he moved most of his belongings into it. After the war he went back to Newport Beach and eventually sold the ranch, which was then developed into the country club. John Wayne's house was used for a while as the clubhouse for the golf course. When it came time to build a new club-house, the parcel on which the house stood was sold to a gentleman from Los Angeles who announced plans to tear down the old building and replace it with a modern edifice. The locals were outraged. No one had thought to put a clause in the contract stipulating that John Wayne's house couldn't be torn down. When they told the new owner whose house he was getting ready to bulldoze, he asked, "Who's John Wayne?" As incredulous as that sounds, he was serious. The next day the bulldozers did their work. This all happened before my application but I have met the gentleman and he is a real pleasant guy. I don't know why he did what he did, but a piece of history is gone.

Getting accepted at Pauma Valley was not exactly the easiest thing that I had ever done. They asked for a long list of references and I believe they checked with every one of them! Our good friend from the days at Parsons, Kansas, Bill Wilson, got a call one day from the membership chairman. Mr. Chairman told Bill that one of his friends had applied for membership and Bill asked which friend? The chairman told him it was Larry and Sue Runyon and Bill says, "You want me to recommend them for membership in your country club?" The chairman says yes and Bill tells him, "Well, I'd have no trouble recommending Sue but I wouldn't let that S.O.B. Larry be a member of any club that I belonged to!" I never have talked my way out of that one, but I was accepted as a member! It was a really big deal when they accepted my application. Here I was this damn superintendent, with a superintendent mentality, and I'm now a member of one of the top golf courses in the world!

I ended up playing regularly with some really great guys. Fritz Swinehart, Bud Barnes, Tom Talbot, John Cartwright and Jim Clark were among the CEO's, company presidents, stockbrokers and other captains of industry that accepted me into their golfing groups and treated me just fine. I really think the world of these guys.

Anyway, that's my story up to this point in my life. There are more tales to tell, some of which I can't tell until the guilty parties are dead, some I have sworn never to tell and some I may just sit down and tell later on. I've seen a lot, done a lot and heard a lot in my 60 years on this old earth. Most of it has been enjoyable or at least semi-funny. I look forward to what the next 60 years has in store.

I guess if I had to choose one sentence to sum it all up, considering everything that I've gotten mixed up in and all of the people and places I've seen, I'd have to go with what the ladies back in Fort Riley, Kansas, said after they got into a fist fight over trophies. When I stepped in to break it up they said, "You burr headed bastard, it's all your fault!" I don't know that I can rightly disagree with that statement!

CPSIA information can be obtained at www.ICGtesting.com
Printed in the USA
BVOW011656220112

281123BV00001B/35/A